550 Perennial Garden Ideas

550 Perennial

A ROUNDTABLE PRESS BOOK

BY DEREK FELL & CAROLYN HEATH

PHOTOGRAPHS BY DEREK FELL

Garden Ideas

SIMON & SCHUSTER

NEW YORK LONDON TORONTO SYDNEY TOKYO SINGAPORE

SIMON & SCHUSTER
Simon & Schuster Building
Rockefeller Center
1230 Avenue of the Americas
New York, New York 10020

A ROUNDTABLE PRESS BOOK
Directors: Susan E. Meyer, Marsha Melnick
Project Editor: Marisa Bulzone
Editor: Anne Halpin
Design: Binns & Lubin/Betty Binns
Layout: Leslie Goldman
Cover Design: Stacey Holston
Color Separations: Oceanic Graphic Printing, Inc.

Printed in Hong Kong

10 9 8 7 6 5 4 3 2 1

LIBRARY OF CONGRESS CATALOGING-IN-PUBLICATION DATA
Fell, Derek.
  550 perennial garden ideas / by Derek Fell & Carolyn Heath;
photographs by Derek Fell.
    p.   cm.
  "A Roundtable Press book."
  Includes index.
  ISBN 0-671-79839-1
  1. Perennials. 2. Perennials—United States. 3. Gardens—Designs
and plans. 4. Gardens—United States—Designs and plans.
I. Heath, Carolyn. II. Title. III. Title: Five hundred fifty
perennial garden ideas.
SB434.F44 1994
716—dc20   93-5525
                                           CIP

Acknowledgments

The authors wish to thank Wendy Fields, grounds superintendent at Cedaridge Farm, for helping to care for so many of the perennial plantings featured in this book, and Kathy Nelson for her efficient management of the extensive color picture library at Cedaridge Farm, from which many of the photographs were selected. The library represents more than fifteen years of garden visitation from coast to coast, and we wish space would allow us to thank the dozens of garden owners for the opportunity to photograph their creations. We are especially indebted to the following design professionals for permission to photograph their work: Kurt Bluemel, Baldwin, Maryland; Brickman Industries, Langhorne, Pennsylvania; Creative Landscaping, Long Island, New York; Kathy Duckett, Plumsteadville, Pennsylvania; Robert Fletcher, Pacific Palisades, California; John Greenlee, Pomona, California; John Harlow, Tucson, Arizona; Hiroshi Makita, Collegeville, Pennsylvania; Oehme, Van Sweden & Associates, Washington D.C.; Plimpton Associates, Ormand Beach, Florida; Dennis Shaw, Santa Barbara, California; Spring Hill Nurseries, Tipp City, Ohio; Carter van Dyke, Doylestown, Pennsylvania; Western Hills Nursery, Occidental, California.

Contents

Introduction

America is having a glorious love affair with perennials—and no wonder! Not only do they introduce a far greater range of design possibilities than annuals, perennials also offer a more sophisticated selection of interesting colors, plant form, and foliage texture.

There is no lack of information about the plants themselves; a dozen or more good perennial books cover growing information, including zones of hardiness, culture, methods of propagation, flowering season, and color range. What the country needs is a book of *ideas,* especially ways to use perennials creatively in different climatic conditions and topographical situations. In particular, there is a need for ideas for *American* gardens, since most other books dealing with design are British-born or use too many pictures and examples from Britain, where the climate is vastly different from that of North America.

Presented here is a feast of perennial garden designs, from coast to coast, gathered over a period of twenty-five years, offered in a clear, organized sequence. The chapters and subcategories identify designs for different parts of the country, and for different soils and environmental conditions. The book recognizes the need to present the vast family of perennials in groups with common characteristics—identifying not only those that are hardy and tender, but also the best perennial bulbs, woody perennials, vines and groundcovers. The book also identifies those perennials that are the most widely adapted, and that consistently provide the greatest satisfaction.

The generally accepted definition of a perennial is any herbaceous plant requiring at least two growing seasons to flower, and living on from year to year. Perennials are more permanent than annuals, which complete their life cycle in one season, and they are longer-lived than biennials, which die after two seasons. Perennials may be as long-lived as many woody plants, particularly small trees and shrubs.

Biennials are usually generous self-seeders, and so they often give the impression of being perennials. This group includes English foxglove (*Digitalis purpurea*), sweet William (*Dianthus barbatus*), and the horned poppy (*Glaucium flavum*). Biennials like these are so beautiful and such an essential part of mixed perennial plantings that this book sides with tradition and considers them perennial.

In other ways, too, the term perennial is sometimes confusing. Refer to a copy of *Hortus III*—the bible on botanical nomenclature in North America—and you will discover that the description often refers to perennial herbs (an herb, in botanical terms, is any perennial plant with soft, nonwoody stems), perennial bulbs, such as daffodils, and even perennial shrubs, such as roses. *Hortus III* also classifies as perennials many plants that are familiar to gardeners as tender annuals, such as flame nettle (*Coleus blumei*), sweet heliotrope (*Heliotropum arboreum*), and kingfisher daisy (*Felicia amelloides*). These plants are actually fast-growing perennials killed by frost. Gardeners in northern states must treat them as annuals, but gardeners in frost-free areas (or gardeners owning a greenhouse) can overwinter them.

There is also a group of plants called *subshrubs,* which bridge the gap between soft-stemmed perennials (known as *herbaceous perennials*) and woody plants, which possess a more durable cell structure called wood). Subshrubs start off with soft stems but develop woody parts with age. English lavender (*Lavandula angustifolia*), perennial candytuft (*Iberis sempervirens*), and tree peonies (*Paeonia suffruticosa*) are examples. Most people regard all these plants as perennials because they look like perennials when young, and because they are most often used in perennial borders.

There is another special group of perennial plants known as *perannuals*. These are hardy perennials that will flower the first year from seed. The hardy hibiscus, *Hibiscus moscheutos* 'Southern Belle', is an excellent example. Started eight weeks before planting outdoors (after frost danger is past), it will begin to flower in early August. Though its foliage is killed by frost, the roots survive even harsh winters, and the plants will re-bloom from year to year.

Perennial bulbs are often differentiated from true perennials because they have an underground storage organ called a bulb. Tulips are a good example of perennial bulbs. Though the bulblike structures have different names depending on their construction (rhizomes, corms, and tubers, for example), all of them are storehouses of energy that enable the plant to survive periods of stress (usually cold winters or drought).

This book takes the position of *Hortus III,* that a perennial is any plant—herbaceous, bulbous, or woody—that will live from year to year. Since most gardeners are interested in flowers, the emphasis is on flowering perennials, and since three-quarters of the United States has at least some snow cover in winter, another emphasis is on hardy kinds. However, popular varieties of tender perennials (especially ice plants and cactus) and perennials grown for their decorative foliage (such as ornamental grasses and ferns) are also included.

The text concentrates on the herbaceous perennials, including perennial bulbs, but I have also included some ideas using small woody plants, such as azaleas and hydrangeas, that are useful in perennial beds and borders.

The diversity of herbaceous perennials allows them to be used in many ways, either alone or combined with annuals and shrubs. Although the most experienced perennial gardeners have been British, it is not wise for Americans to slavishly follow British design and planting recommendations. The British experience milder winters than most of North America, and many plants that they describe as hardy simply perish in North America's harsh winters or burn up during the summer's heat. Also, during summer the British enjoy more comfortable temperatures and more frequent rainfall than most of the United States. While North American gardeners may experience difficulty growing such popular British perennial fare as blue poppies (*Meconopsis grandis*) and candelabra primroses (*Primula bulleyana*), the British rarely succeed with such wonderful North American perennials as butterfly weed (*Asclepias tuberosa*), trumpet creeper (*Campsis radicans*), and swamp hibiscus (*Hibiscus moscheutos*), all of which relish warm, sunny summers. Pictorially, therefore, this book presents perennial planting ideas found mostly in North American gardens.

However, on the question of design principles, it is a good idea to respect some of the theories presented by such knowledgeable European gardeners as the British gardening expert Gertrude

▶

Cushion chrysanthemums are a "quick fix" for any bare garden spaces in autumn. This mixed planting occupies a bed that changes with the seasons. The plants are purchased locally in a ready-to-bloom stage. They survive light frosts and bloom well into late fall. After flowering, this display is dug up, and the plants spotted about the property, where they often endure even harsh winters to rebloom.

Jekyll and the famous French Impressionist painter Claude Monet. This is particularly true in the creation of color harmonies and the management of color contrasts.

Miss Jekyll's reputation as an eminent garden designer solidified when she teamed up with one of Europe's most talented architects, Sir Edwin Lutyens, who liked to surround the homes he designed with a garden that could be identified as an extension of the house. Lutyens designed the "hardscape"—pergolas, walls, water features, walks, and courtyards—to blend with the house (often in consultation with Miss Jekyll), while Miss Jekyll designed the "softscape," using mostly herbaceous perennials. British garden historian Richard Bisgrove, author of *The Gardens of Gertrude Jekyll* (Little, Brown & Co.), notes that "Miss Jekyll's naturalistic planting wedded Lutyens's geometry in a balanced union of both principles." She shared garden writer William Robinson's enthusiasm for innovative plantings and started contributing to his progressive garden magazine, *The Garden;* she also wrote parts of his popular book, *The English Flower Garden* (Saga Press), which stresses the importance of plants more than the structures in landscape design. Jekyll's own books influenced many great gardeners, among them Vita Sackville-West (who created the famous gardens at Sissinghurst), Graham Stuart Thomas (garden adviser to the British National Trust), Princess Greta Sturdza (owner of the French woodland garden Le Vasterival), and Constance Spry (eminent British floral arranger).

This homage to European gardeners is not meant to imply, however, that North America lacks outstanding perennial gardening experts of its own. In the Northeast, the beautiful estate garden of Wave Hill, off the Henry Hudson Parkway, in The Bronx, New York, under the energetic direction of Marco Polo Stufano, features several theme gardens using primarily

Create a monochromatic yellow color harmony in spring by combining the yellow Triandrus hybrid daffodil Hawera with a fragrant Ghent hybrid azalea. The Ghent hybrids were developed from North American species such as *Rhododendron calendulaceum,* which is native to the Blue Ridge Mountains. They are similar to Exbury azaleas but have a less hybridized look, so they are more suitable for woodland gardens.

perennials, presented in sophisticated color harmonies as good as any that the British can offer. Though the harmonies and contrasts are in the spirit of Jekyll, the plant combinations are refreshingly original, and many examples of Wave Hill's innovative perennial plantings are presented in this book.

The trailblazing design firm of Oehme, Van Sweden & Associates, headquartered in Washington, D.C., is successful because of the teamwork of two landscape architects: Wolfgang Oehme, who mostly chooses the plants, and James Van Sweden, who executes most of the designs. Their partnership is not unlike that of Jekyll and Lutyens.

The beautiful California estate garden of Filoli, near Woodside—just south of San Francisco—shows the skills of a partnership between Isabella Worn, a plantsperson, and Bruce Porter, whom the owner entrusted with the overall garden design.

By profession, Bruce Porter was an artist, impressed by Miss Worn's sense of color and knowledge of plants suitable for the Mediterranean-like California climate. For his client—a wealthy expatriate Irishman—he designed a large, walled garden reminiscent of Irish country estates, but filled with connecting "garden rooms"—outdoor spaces enclosed by hedges and walls. This successful collaboration was repeated in several other California gardens. Pictures of Miss Worn inspecting her work at Filoli show a stout, conservatively dressed woman with a resemblance to Queen Victoria; she could easily be mistaken for Gertrude Jekyll.

Farther up the coast, in the Pacific Northwest, the climate more closely resembles that of the British Isles (see Chapter 3, "Regional Differences"). Here thrive many of the more temperamental British perennials, such as the giant Himalayan trumpet lily (*Cardiocrinum giganticum*) and the giant gunnera (*Gunnera manicata*). Just across the Canadian border, in Vancouver, is the beautiful Van Dusen Botanical Garden. Formerly a golf course slated for development, it is now a spacious botanical garden famous for its perennial plantings. Just a few hours' drive south from Van Dusen, in Washington State, is perhaps the world's most beautiful rock garden, Oehme Gardens. Located high on a rocky promontory overlooking the agricultural community of Wenatchee, it is a lavishly planted alpine garden featuring a rich assortment of hardy perennials massed along a labyrinth of stone paths and steps. The paths penetrate groves of Douglas fir and criss-cross alpine meadows threaded with cascading streams.

Perhaps the most exciting prospect in perennial gardening in North America is the opportunity for innovation. American gardeners have different climatic conditions to work with and different environmental surroundings to draw inspiration from than their counterparts in England. The wonderful perennial garden of Western Hills in Occidental, California, is unique for its location within a redwood forest; the historic garden of Magnolia Plantation near Charleston, South Carolina, works within a cypress swamp, with bald cypress trees so old you half expect to see a dinosaur wading through the lakes; at Leamings Run, a trail garden in Swainton, New Jersey, theme gardens are nestled within natural stands of holly, pine, ferns, pitcher plants, and waterlilies—all native to the low-lying coastal wilderness.

There is also a richer plant palette when one looks at the natural North American landscape and considers endemic plants that are often taken for granted—especially prairie wildflowers such as the *Liatris* and *Oenothera* species. Though Europeans have long been familiar with the beauty of ornamental grasses, never have grasses been used as imaginatively as in the designs of ornamental grass experts Kurt Bluemel and Wolfgang Oehme on the East Coast, or Isabelle Green and Robert Fletcher on the West Coast. Taking inspiration from the great western deserts and midwestern prairies, these talented garden designers use grasses and succulent plants in great sweeps to create gentle waves of color soothing to the senses.

Nowhere is the strength of native North American wildflowers seen more clearly than in the fifty-acre hillside garden of the Henry Foundation near Gladwyn, Pennsylvania. There, from a Tudor-style house resembling the Royal Horticultural Society headquarters at Wisley, England, Josephine Henry heads a dedicated staff that carries on the work of her late mother, who traversed the American wilderness in search of hardy wildflowers with ornamental value. Three principal areas—a rock scree, a sunny meadow, and a shady woodland—harbor native American wildflowers in beautiful companion plantings. The plants were gathered from the wild because they exhibited some special trait, such as a richer coloration or a more floriferous habit of growth. Native lilies, pink yuccas, purple phlox, white gayfeathers, silvery sedums, cantaloupe-colored trumpet creepers, fragrant orange deciduous azaleas, yellow honeysuckles, and deep blue false indigo are just a sampling of the plants that have been collected from the wild, and that exhibit superior color and forms. Plants are available to gardeners who join the foundation.

This book seeks to present as diverse a selection of design ideas as possible, using both familiar and unfamiliar plants in good color harmonies and interesting companion plantings. It also seeks to present designs that are not only formal or informal but, in some cases, a successful marriage of the two.

Chapter One

Gardening With Perennials

Our home, Cedaridge Farm, in Bucks County, Pennsylvania, dates back to 1790. When we first moved here the land around the stone farmhouse was mostly lawns shaded with mature sugar maples, sloping down to a stream and a pond. In a space of just three years, the site blossomed with ten major theme gardens, using mostly perennial plants for ornamental effect. The overall design philosophy at Cedaridge is to maintain an old-fashioned appearance, using not only old-fashioned plant varieties but also old construction materials, including rusty iron gates, fieldstone for retaining walls, Pennsylvania black slate for roofing, and even stepping-stone paths. Above all, we follow the design philosophies of that great Victorian perennial expert Gertrude Jekyll, who created a renowned garden at her home, Munstead Wood, in the south of England, and led the way into a world of less formality in planting and more imaginative color harmonies. Like that of Munstead Wood, the garden at Cedaridge Farm blends with the surrounding woodland. The garden flows gradually from the dramatic color of flowering garden varieties to the soft, soothing greens of indigenous plant life beyond the cultivated spaces.

Following Jekyll's example, we use special areas for a particular plant family, when the plant family provides enough interest and a sufficiently wide color range. In particular, we have a sunny rose garden that leans heavily on old garden varieties for a romantic look, a sunny border of Michaelmas daisies (autumn-flowering asters), an ornamental-grass garden that is especially beautiful in autumn, and a sheltered peony garden that features both herbaceous peonies and the earlier flowering tree peonies.

In her most famous herbaceous borders, Jekyll grouped plants in color zones, beginning at the lower end with cool colors mixed with silvery foliage. In the center of the border, the colors strengthened to include yellows and orange through red and crimson, the darkest

reds subdued by the proximity of plants with bronze foliage. The colors would then recede to cooler tones again and more silver foliage. Many of her color harmonies were inspired by Impressionist paintings, and she was called the world's first Impressionist horticulturist (though in my opinion it is Claude Monet who is more deserving of that title). Like Gertrude Jekyll, I am a garden photographer, and many of the garden spaces are planted so I can capture for publication images of special planting schemes and fleeting atmospheric conditions, such as the effects of rain, mist, frost, and snow.

The Importance of Good Soil

None of these marvelous plantings—at either Cedaridge or Munstead Wood—would have been possible without good soil, and perhaps more than any other plant category, perennials do like a deep, fertile soil. Many perennials are greedy feeders and dwindle in a thin, impoverished, or poorly drained soil. When starting a new perennial border, Jekyll would instruct her gardeners to dig down to a depth of four feet, mixing in cartloads of well-decomposed animal manures. She was also fastidious about composting and using good

tools, believing a solidly built wheelbarrow (for hauling compost) and a strong, sharp Sheffield steel spade (for digging) to be the two most useful tools in her garden.

◄

A perennial bed in the process of being dug where previously there was only lawn. Before the indigenous soil can be improved, the turf grass must be removed completely.

Since the Jekyll years, there have been many innovations in plant varieties, and also in tools and fertilizer, allowing the modern perennial gardener not only a broader plant palette, but also the means to ensure faster results. Following is a step-by-step procedure for cultivating perennials and for their continuing care.

Location

With a spade, walk around your property and learn its strengths and weaknesses. Draw a plan showing its soil composition (areas of hard clay, sand, rock, humus-rich loam, or leaf mold), its hydrology (dry spots, wet spots, direction of drainage, streams, ponds, boggy places, and—most important—water sources such as water spigots and/or wells), and its microclimates (frost pockets, sun traps, shady areas, sheltered spaces, and the direction of the prevailing winds).

Develop one area at a time, and decide one strong design theme for each space, matching the theme to the habitat. For example, an herb garden needs especially good drainage and sunlight; a spring bulb garden can tolerate light shade providing the bulbs have a humus-rich soil. Consider a strong garden accent to complement the plants: a sundial for the herb garden, a bench among the spring-flowering bulbs, a bridge over a stream, stepping stones through a boggy area, or a gazebo in a rose garden. Don't overdo the structures, or your property may start to look like a miniature golf course.

Always consider plant hardiness. Learn what hardiness zone you live in, and choose plants recommended for that zone. In sheltered spaces, you may want to experiment with plants from a warmer zone.

Soil Preparation

If you don't know the nature of your soil, have it tested. Your local county agent will provide you with instructions on how to submit a soil sample. The report that the soil laboratory sends back to you will say whether you have acid, alkaline, or neutral soil, what its nutrient content is, and other vital statistics. The report will also tell you how to correct any imbalance.

Most perennials grow best in a neutral or slightly acid soil. If your soil is overly acid, the report will tell you exactly how much lime to apply, and how often. If it is too alkaline, the report will tell you how much sulfur to add. If there is any nutrient deficiency, the report will tell you how much nitrogen, phosphorus, or potash to add, and also if any trace elements—such as calcium—are missing.

A trug containing some basic tools for planting perennials. Pruners can be used to trim broken roots before planting, gloves protect hands from scratches, and the hand fork is for digging planting holes.

Gertrude Jekyll never had the benefit of a scientific soil test, and her soil analysis consisted of feeling the soil with her hands. If the soil slipped through her fingers easily in granules, it was judged to be sandy with poor moisture-holding capacity, and if it squeezed into a cold, dense lump, she knew it was clay and impervious to plant roots. If it was fluffy and friable, it was loam, the best kind of garden soil—a mixture of sand, clay, silt, and humus. An auger or spade could be used to determine the depth of any good topsoil. When topsoil is thin, sandy, or clay, humus must be added. Today, when stables and dairies are scarce and well-decomposed animal manures are unavailable, good alternative soil conditioners include garden compost, composted leaves, spent mushroom soil, and horticultural peat. Where poor soils cannot be dug deeply because of an impervious subsoil, such as shale or caliche, you can increase your soil's depth by creating a raised bed with stones or brick. Where aesthetic considerations are unimportant, also consider landscape ties.

Planting Perennials

Many store-bought hardy perennials can be planted at any time during the growing season, especially if they have been grown in pots such as one-gallon containers.

Perennial plants purchased from mail-order sources may be small, bare-root plants or cuttings with a meager root system. Before transferring these directly to your garden, you may wish to plant them in pots, or a special nursery bed, and hold them for a month or two in a sheltered area until their root system has filled out. The same is true if you buy perennials in flats from local garden centers. A flat may contain 32 small perennial plants (usually seed-grown), and this is an inexpensive way to obtain a lot of plants for your garden.

Proper spacing is important. Small perennials, such as forget-me-nots and evening primroses, will tolerate crowding and can be planted twelve inches apart, like annuals. Larger perennials, such as daylilies, bearded irises, and shasta daisies, will need more room—usually two-and-a-half to three feet apart. If any bare soil is left after you plant perennials at the proper spacing, you can fill it with annuals such as nasturtiums, French marigolds, and alyssum.

To plant potted perennials, slide the root ball out of the pot gently, retaining as much soil around the roots as possible. Bury the root ball so the top is level with the surrounding soil

Example of a dwarf bearded iris purchased from a local garden center in a gallon container. The plant is in bloom and ready to add instant color to the garden.

▼

Perennials in three-inch pots are less expensive than those in gallon containers and are generally preferred for creating large beds. These are Scottish heather transplants.

▼

A perennial garden planted completely with plants purchased by mail order, in early May. For a view of what this garden looked like just three months later, in mid-July, see page 102.

▲

A wheelbarrow loaded with plants purchased by mail from a reliable nursery. The plants in the plastic flat are mostly healthy young seedlings, grown in small pots. Those in plastic bags are older plants, mostly supplied bare-root. Some have green tops, but others are still dormant, and no green growth is visible.

surface, fill in around the sides with topsoil, water, and the soil, and tamp it down so there is good soil contact with the root ball.

Before planting bare-root perennials, tease the roots apart, and sprinkle soil between the roots so they are not tangled or matted. Position each plant so it fits snugly in its planting hole, sitting not too high and not too low. Water, and tamp down the soil with your foot to ensure good soil contact.

Watering

The best investment any home gardener can make is an irrigation system, which keeps a perennial garden from being at the mercy of natural rainfall. In small gardens, it's easy enough to use lawn sprinklers, allowing them to operate for several hours before moving them to another location. However, in large gardens, a subsurface drip irrigation system can save a lot of time. Beds and borders that are shaded do not need as much watering as those in a sunny loca-

▲

The easiest and most inexpensive way to water large plantings of perennials is with a lawn sprinkler. This unit has been set high on an overturned pot and anchored in place with a stone so it can reach a planting of Enchantment Asiatic hybrid lilies. Watering with overhead sprinklers is inexpensive, but not as efficient as watering with subsurface drip irrigation.

tion. Also, beds that are mulched with an organic material—such as shredded leaves and wood chips—do not dry out as quickly as beds that expose bare soil.

Pest Control

Pests and diseases most often attack weak plants. With only a few exceptions (roses and some exotic lilies), most perennials are tough and trouble-free—and it is possible to have a beautiful perennial garden without resorting to poisonous chemical sprays.

Among insect pests, the most troublesome are generally beetles, nematodes, caterpillars, and snails (or slugs). Milky spore bacterial control is an effective, nonpolluting way to rid your property of Japanese beetles, which love rose blossoms and hibiscus foliage. Milky spore is sprinkled over the garden in spring, enters the soil, and attacks Japanese beetle larvae before they emerge as adults.

Destructive caterpillars are controlled by BT (*Bacillus thuringiensis*), a bacterial disease that attacks only caterpillars.

Nematodes are microscopic worms (called *eel worms*) that are most prevalent in warm, sandy soils. They are especially destructive of lilies and other summer-flowering bulbs. New beds can be sterilized by solar sterilization, that is, the placement of a clear plastic sheet over newly dug soil, which allows the sun's heat to scorch the earth and kill off harmful nematodes.

You can control slugs and snails by eliminating places for them to hide—especially under boards and loose stones—or also by hand picking an area in the early morning. Dusting the ground with wood ashes and diatomaceous earth will also control snails.

►

Many hardy perennials are tempting to deer. Since the owner of this garden is not able to fence deer out of his property, he has covered a planting of azaleas, holly, and tulips with bird netting. Perennials are most vulnerable during autumn, winter, and early spring, when food in the wild is scarce.

Large pests—such as deer, groundhogs, and rodents—are more easily controlled than insect pests. To keep deer out of the garden, you generally need high fencing. Also, there are odorless deer repellents that can be sprayed on ornamental plants to make them distasteful. Groundhogs must be trapped with baited cages and removed far away. Rodent populations can be controlled to some extent by cats, but even so, rodents can take a heavy toll of tasty bulbs, such as tulips, and of roses. At the onset of winter, rake mothballs into the upper soil surface around susceptible plants, and delay applying a protective mulch until the ground has frozen.

Staking

You can reduce the chore of staking tall perennials by choosing dwarf varieties. For example, in good soil, the obedient plant (*Physostegia virginica*) will grow to five feet and flop all over the place, but the dwarf variety 'Vivid' stays neat and compact at little more than three feet. Similarly, the dwarf shasta daisy 'Silver Princess' will form a tidy cushion that requires no staking. However, in the best perennial borders, tall plants are desirable for the back of the border, and staking is needed to keep them erect.

Enterprising garden-supply houses have introduced an array of supports, but generally it's hard to beat the old-fashioned bamboo cane, with its raised circular leaf nodes that stop string or twist ties from slipping. Of course, tying plant stems to canes takes time, and there are now wire supports that allow perennials to be self-supporting. These have a circular grid raised on three or four splayed legs so that growing stems can poke through. For supporting vines, wooden trellis is aesthetically the most pleasing. It can be laid flat against a wall or built into decorative structures, such as arches and arbors.

◄

This sturdy wire support is specially made to help support the stems of tall perennials, particularly peonies. The feet simply press into the soil, and a wide wire mesh allows the sprouting shoots to push through the mesh and become self-supporting.

Fertilizing

The nutrient that benefits perennials the most is phosphorus. It is present in packaged fertilizers that have a high middle number in their formula, such as 10–20–10, and in bone meal, an organic fertilizer made from crushed animal bones. For large plantings (such as mass plantings of daffodils and garden lilies), bone meal is expensive, but an economical substitute is superphosphate.

Phosphorus builds strong roots and also stimulates flowering. Nitrogen benefits leafy growth, and potash is necessary for extra vigor and disease resistance.

For the best results, feed perennial plantings twice a year: in spring, before any vigorous new growth begins, and then again in autumn, after frost. If you have time to feed only once, do it in the autumn.

A well-made compost pile can provide all the nutrients your perennials will need, but it's faster to use a granular commercial fertilizer. For the correct rate of application, read the label, as different brands have different formulas. Some fertilizers work quickly because their crystals of nutrient dissolve in water. They can be applied with ease to the root zone through a spray applicator attached to a garden hose. Most professional growers prefer to use a timed-release fertilizer, as one application is sufficient to last all season. Pellets containing nutrients are sprinkled over the soil surface around plants, and they slowly dissolve, releasing the nutrients over several months.

Weed Control

It is essential to remove weed roots from newly dug soil, and to prevent weed seeds from contaminating established beds. Even a small piece of dandelion root or wild morning-glory root can regenerate, so it is essential to clear a soil completely of every tiny section of weed root. Once a bed has been cleared of weeds and planted with perennials, it is best to place a layer of mulch over the bare sections of soil to suffocate weed seedlings and to act as a barrier against new seeds that are blown onto the site. Some excellent mulches to consider are shredded leaves, pine needles, and shredded pine bark. If mulches are to stay effective, they should be topped-up as soon as natural decomposition exposes any bare patches of soil.

To prevent intrusion from nearby weeds, keep surrounding areas weed-free. Where weeds grow tall on a nearby meadow or waste site, mow them down before their seeds have a chance to ripen. In difficult-to-mow areas, use a weed whacker. High hedges and walls act as an additional barrier to contamination from weed seeds.

▼

This perennial border has been mulched with shredded pine bark not only to suffocate weeds, but also to conserve soil moisture. Mulching also helps to protect plants from damage during alternate winter freezes and thaws.

◄ To prevent damage to the canes of climbing roses during winter, tie the canes securely to strong supports; flapping canes can easily dehydrate in cold winds.

Winter Protection

Where winters are severe, and the ground may be subjected to alternate freezing and thawing, even hardy perennials will benefit from a layer of organic mulch placed around their roots. This mulch should be applied after the ground freezes so that mice have a chance to build their winter nests elsewhere, and because the main objective of a protective mulch is to keep the ground frozen and the plants dormant until a prolonged spring thaw really arrives. Otherwise, plants may be fooled into breaking dormancy and then suffer winterkill when a hard freeze returns.

Except for perennial vines, it is best to cut the topgrowth of most perennials to within several inches of the ground after a hard frost. This process helps tidy up the planting spaces and allows mulch to be applied more easily.

Perennial bulbs considered too tender for overwintering—such as dahlias and gladiolus—should be dug up and brushed clean of soil, then allowed to cure (dry in the sun for a day or two), after which they should be moved indoors into a cool, frost-free area. Any tender perennials you have used as special accents in tubs (such as angel's trumpets and banana trees) should be taken indoors before the first fall frost.

Deer become bolder in the winter, and unless a covering of bird netting is stretched over the beds and borders, they can inflict damage on perennial beds by digging up tender roots and bulbs with their hooves.

▼

For the mass production of perennial plants, hoop houses are essential because they allow a large number of perennials to be sheltered under plastic during freezing weather. Many hardy perennials require no artificial heat, just a covering of plastic during severe weather to keep them safe and to encourage strong growth.

Propagation by Division

Some perennials—such as beebalm and yarrow—may be so aggressive that they outgrow their allotted space after just two seasons. When this happens, division is essential—not only to keep the design in balance, but to stop weaker perennials from being completely crowded out.

Division is also normally possible at any time during the growing season (though most gardeners prefer to divide perennials after they have finished flowering). However, the best time is usually in the fall, so that the divisions can create a generous root system to support extra-vigorous topgrowth in spring. Use a sharp spade to completely

◄ A clump of shasta daisies showing small root divisions pulled from the mother plant. Each division will grow a plant identical to the parent and, within three years, will require division again to keep the plant from spreading outside its allocated space.

dig up the root mass. Once the entire root mass is lifted out of the ground, you can hose it down to dislodge earth and make the mass easier to divide into smaller sections. Some perennials—such as hostas and daylilies—are easily hand-separated once the soil is removed from around the roots, but more aggressive perennials, such as eulalia grass (*Miscanthus sinensis*), may be so dense that a sharp spade or a chain saw will be needed to divide the tightly knit roots into smaller clumps.

After division, you can replant the original space with a smaller clump of the same plant unless you want to substitute something else. Large divisions can be planted in other parts of the garden, but smaller divisions are best potted up into gallon-capacity containers and kept in a lightly shaded area until they have filled out their root systems and topgrowth.

Some aggressive bulbs—such as daffodils—may also need dividing after three years; otherwise they tend to produce more leafy growth than flowers. Simply dig these up in the autumn, separate the crowded bulbs, and replant at least three inches apart.

► Bearded-iris divisions produced by dividing the mother plant. For a flowering display the following year growers prefer to plant clumps with at least two fans (clumps of leaves) showing, since one fan may produce only one flower stalk, or none at all, the first season after planting.

◄ A mass of bearded-iris rhizomes ready for division. A garden fork or spade can be used to dig up the oversized clump, known as the mother plant. Divisions can be made anytime after flowering, but preferably in late summer or early autumn.

▲ An example of a new flower bed planted with bearded-iris divisions. Each clump is spaced twelve to fifteen inches apart. Annuals can be used to fill in the spaces between the newly divided plants until they grow to fill the bed.

Starting From Seed

The least expensive way to propagate a lot of perennials is from seed. A single packet of seed can produce hundreds of plants for pennies apiece. The back of a seed packet will give instructions for germination.

Generally, seed is best sown in a seed tray, with a heating cable underneath to provide "bottom heat." Peat-based potting soils with a moisture-holding gel are best, though succulents prefer a sandy potting soil. A clear plastic cover over the seed tray will help to maintain a moist microclimate. Make sure that the seed tray has good overall light. Light from one direction—such as a window-sill—can make seedlings stretch and can weaken them. Potting soils and seed trays must be clean: otherwise a soil fungus disease called *damping off* may cause seedlings to wilt and die.

When the seedlings are large enough to handle, transfer them to individual pots. Feed them with a dilute liquid fertilizer every two weeks until the plants fill the pot. Then transfer them to the garden.

► Many kinds of perennials can be started from seed. They are first sown in seed trays (center), filled with a peat-based potting medium, and covered with clear plastic to prevent rapid drying out of the medium. After germination, the seedlings can be transferred to individual peat pots (left) and, if necessary, into larger pots (right) before they are transplanted into the garden.

Some perennials grown from seed will vary, depending on variety, and if you want an exact match in color and habit, it may be better to consider division or cuttings. In particular, the seed of hybrids may be sterile and may produce nothing, or the progeny may be considerably inferior to the parent.

Create New Plants From Cuttings

Carnations are the best example of a perennial that is easily propagated by stem cuttings. Carnations will root just below a leaf node when a four- to six-inch section of stem is cut and the cut end is inserted in a moist potting soil.

Sedums are an example of perennials that are easily propagated by leaf cuttings. Simply snap off a leaf where it meets the stem and insert the broken end in moist potting soil. You can increase your rate of success from stem cuttings and leaf cuttings if you dip the cut end first in rooting hormone, a white powder available from garden centers.

Oriental poppies are the best example of a perennial that can be increased by root cuttings. When you dig up a clump of poppy roots, you will see small pointed nodes spaced at regular intervals along the fleshy roots. Simply take a sharp knife, cut each root into three-inch sections with a node included, and cover the sections with potting soil. The node will quickly sprout green topgrowth, and the submerged root section will explode with feeder roots.

Other Methods of Propagation

A few perennials have developed some uncommon methods of propagation. For example, many garden lilies develop black bulbils in their leaf axils. These can be pulled off and planted like seeds; they will create an exact replica of the parent. Hardy begonias (*Begonia grandis*) and some tropical waterlilies are viviparous, growing exact miniatures of themselves from their leaves. These babies can be removed and potted up to grow into useful transplants.

► Perennials started from seed and those growing from cuttings or divisions should be held in a shaded area until ready for transplanting into the garden. This lathe house not only provides the necessary shelter from direct sun but has raised beds that can be covered with clear plastic for protection from freezing weather.

Amortizing Your Costs

Gertrude Jekyll was able to employ nine gardeners to take care of her garden by running a nursery on the side and selling plants to her clients. Rosemary Verey, owner of a successful perennial garden in England, is able to maintain her large garden by selling plants. Some garden owners even develop a specialized mail-order business by selling plants. The propagating areas and the display areas are kept quite separate. The propagating areas not only pay the bills but are a source of new plants for the garden.

18 Perennials for Special Purposes

The following are some lists of perennials suitable for special purposes. They are mostly herbaceous perennials featured in this book, including perennial bulbs. Varieties marked with an asterisk (*) are tender (sensitive to freezing temperatures).

Drought Tolorence
*Tender

Botanical name	Common name
Achillea filipendulina	Yellow yarrow
Aloe striata *	Showy aloe
Anigozanthus flavidus *	Kangaroo paw
Anthemis tinctoria	Yellow marguerite
Arabis caucasica	Rock cress
Armeria maritima	Thrift
Artemisia ludoviciana	Wormwood
Asclepias tuberosa	Butterfly weed
Aurinia saxatilis	Perennial alyssum
Callirhoe species	Poppy mallow
Campanula persicifolia	Willow-leaf bellflower
Catanache caerulea	Cupid's dart
Cerastium tomentosum	Snow-in-summer
Cistus ladanifer *	Rock rose
Coreopsis lanceolata	Lance-leaf coreopsis
C. verticillata	Thread-leaf coreopsis
Cortaderia selloana *	Pampas plume
Dianthus plumarius	Cottage pinks
Echinacea purpurea	Purple coneflower
Echinops ritro	Globe thistle
Echium fastuosum *	Pride of Madeira
Epimedium grandiflorum	Bishop's hat
Eryngium giganteum	Sea holly
Euphorbia epithymoides	Cushion spurge
Festuca ovina glauca	Blue fescue
Gaillardia x *grandiflora*	Blanket flower
Gypsophila paniculata	Baby's breath
Helianthemum nummularium	Sun rose
Hemerocallis hybrids	Daylily
Iberis sempervirens	Perennial candytuft
Kniphofia uvaria	Red hot poker
Lavandula angustifolia	English lavender
Leontopodium alpinum	Edelweiss
Liatris spicata	Gayfeather
Linum perenne	Blue flax
Lychnis chalcedonica	Maltese cross
Opuntia humifusa	Hardy prickly pear
Pennisetum setaceum *	Fountain grass
Potentilla fruticosa	Bush cinquefoil
Ratibida columnifera	Prairie coneflower
Salvia x 'Alan Chittering' *	San Diego salvia
S. leucantha *	Mexican sage
Santolina chamaecyparissus	Lavender cotton
Saponaria ocymoides	Soapwort
Sedum species	Stonecrop
Solidago species	Goldenrod
Veronica longifolia	Speedwell
Yucca filamentosa	Spanish dagger

Groundcovers
*Tender

Botanical name	Common name
Aegopodium podograria 'Variegatum' *	Bishop's weed
Agapanthus africanus *	African lily
Ajuga reptans	Bugle weed
Alchemilla mollis	Lady's mantle
Anemone pulsatilla	Pasqueflower
Arctotheca calendula *	Cape marigold
Armeria maritima	Thrift
Bergenia cordifolia	Heart-leaf bergenia
Ceanothus grisius var. *horizontalis* *	Carmel creeper
Cerastium tomentosum	Snow-in-summer
Chamaemelum nobile	Chamomile
Convallaria majalis	Lily of the valley
Coronilla varia	Crown vetch
Drosanthemum roseum	Rosy ice plant
Epimedium grandiflorum	Bishop's hat
Euonymus fortunei	Winter creeper
Gazania rigens var. *leucolaena* *	Trailing gazania
Hemerocallis fulva	Wayside daylily
Hosta sieboldiana	Plantain lily
Hypericum calycinum	St.-John's-wort
Iberis sempervirens	Perennial candytuft
Iris cristata	Crested iris
Lampranthus spectabilis *	Ice plant
Lantana montevidensis	Weeping lantana
Lathyrus latifolius	Perennial sweet pea
Liriope muscari	Lilyturf
Matteuccia struthiopteris	Ostrich plume fern
Myosotis scorpioides	Forget-me-not
Opuntia humifusa	Hardy prickly pear
Osteospermum fruticosum *	Trailing African daisy
Pelargonium peltatum *	Ivy-leaf geranium
Polemonium reptans	Jacob's ladder
Potentilla fruticosa	Bush cinquefoil
Primula vulgaris	English primrose
Sedum species	Stonecrop
Trachelospermum jasminoides *	Confederate jasmine
Vinca minor	Periwinkle

Shade Tolerance
*Tender

Botanical name	Common name
Allium neapolitanum	White allium
Anemone nemorosa	Wood anemone
Aquilegia species and hybrids	Columbine
Arisaema triphyllum	Jack-in-the-pulpit
Arum italicum	Italian arum
Aruncus dioicus	Goatsbeard
Asarum species	Wild ginger
Astilbe x arendsii	False spiraea
Begonia x tuberhybrida	Tuberous begonia
Bergenia cordifolia	Heart-leaf bergenia
Brunnera macrophylla	False forget-me-not
Caladium x hortulanum *	Fancy-leaved caladium
Cardiocrinum giganteum *	Himalayan lily
Cimicifuga racemosa	Black snakeroot
Clivia miniata	Kaffir lily
Convallaria majalis	Lily of the valley
Cyclamen neopolitanum	Hardy cyclamen
Dicentra eximia	Fringed bleeding heart
D. formosa	Pacific bleeding heart
D. spectabilis	Japanese bleeding heart
Digitalis purpurea	English foxglove
Dodecatheon media	Shooting star
Doronicum cordatum	Leopard's-bane
Endymion hispanicus	Spanish bluebell
Epimedium grandiflorum	Bishop's hat
Erythronium 'Pagoda'	Dogtooth violet
Gentiana asclepiadea	Autumn gentian
Helleborus niger	Christmas rose
H. orientalis	Lenten rose
Hesperis matronalis	Sweet rocket
Hosta species and hybrids	Hosta, Plantain lily
Iris foetidissima	Stinking iris
Kalmia latifolia	Mountain laurel
Lamium maculatum	Dead nettle
Leucojum aestivum	Summer snowflake
Lilium species and hybrids	Garden lilies
Liriope species	Lilyturf
Lunaria annua	Money plant
Meconopsis grandis	Blue poppy
Mertensia virginica	Virginia bluebell
Pachysandra terminalis	Japanese spurge
Phlox divaricata	Blue phlox
Podophyllum peltatum	May apple
Polygonatum odoratum	Solomon's seal
Primula x polyantha	Polyanthus primrose
Pulmonaria angustifolia	Lungwort
Rhododendron species	Azalea and rhododendron
Smilacina racemosa	False Solomon's seal
Tiarella cordifolia	Foamflower
Trillium grandiflorum	Wake-robin
Uvularia grandiflora	Bellwort
Vinca minor	Periwinkle
Viola tricolor	Johnny-jump-up

Ferns

Most ferns are shade loving. The following are especially good for woodland gardens.
*Tender

Botanical name	Common name
Adiantum pedatum	Maidenhair fern
Athyrium goeringianum 'Pictum'	Japanese painted fern
Dicksonia antarctica *	Australian tree fern
Matteuccia struthiopteris	Ostrich fern
Woodwardia radicans *	Chain fern

Edging
*Tender

Botanical name	Common name
Anemone blanda	Windflower
Arabis caucasica	Rock cress
Armeria maritima	Thrift
Astilbe chinensis 'Pumila'	Dwarf astilbe
Aubrieta deltoidea	False rock cress
Aurinia saxatilis	Perennial alyssum
Bergenia cordifolia	Heart-leaf bergenia
Campanula portenschlagiana	Dalmatian bellflower
C. poscharskyana	Siberian bellflower
Cerastium tomentosum	Snow-in-summer
Ceratostigma plumbaginoides	Blue plumbago
Convallaria majalis	Lily of the valley
Dianthus plumarius	Cottage pinks
Echeveria elegans *	Mexican snowball
Gaillardia x grandiflora 'Goblin'	Dwarf blanket flower
Hosta 'Wahoo'	Dwarf plantain lily
Iberis sempervirens	Perennial candytuft
Leucanthemum x superbum 'Ms. Muffet'	Dwarf shasta daisy
Liriope muscari	Lilyturf
Myosotis scorpioides	Forget-me-not
Nepeta mussinii	Ornamental catmint
Ophiopogon japonicus	Mondo grass
Phlox subulata	Mountain pinks

Polemonium reptans	Jacob's ladder
Polygonum bistorta	Knotweed
Saxifraga urbium	London pride
Sedum kamtschaticum	Dwarf sedum
S. rubrotinctum *	Ruby sedum
S. 'Weihenstephaner Gold'	Dwarf sedum
Stachys byzantina	Lamb's ears
Viola tricolor	Johnny-jump-up

Boggy Soil

*Tender

Botanical name	Common name
Alchemilla mollis	Lady's mantle
Anaphalis triplinervis	Pearly everlasting
Astilbe x arendsii	False spiraea
Bergenia cordifolia	Heart-leaf bergenia
Calla palustris	Bog arum
Caltha palustris	Marsh marigold
Canna ehmannii *	Water canna
Colocasia esculenta *	Elephant's ears
Geum rivale	Water avens
Gunnera manicata *	Giant gunnera
Helenium autumnale	Sneezeweed
Helianthus x multiflorus	Swamp sunflower
Hibiscus moscheutos	Rose mallow
Hosta species and hybrids	Hosta, Plantain lily
Iris ensata	Japanese iris
I. pseudacorus	Yellow flag iris
I. sibirica	Siberian iris
Ligularia x przewalskii	Rocket ligularia
Lobelia cardinalis	Scarlet lobelia, cardinal flower
L. siphilitica	Blue lobelia
Lysichiton americanum	Yellow skunk cabbage
Lysimachia punctata	Yellow loosestrife
L. salicaria	Purple loosestrife
Matteuccia struthiopteris	Ostrich fern
Monarda didyma	Beebalm
Myosotis scorpioides	Forget-me-not
Petasites japonica	Butterburr
Polygonum bistorta 'Superbum'	Knotweed
Pontederia cordata	Pickerel weed
Primula florindae *	Himalayan cowslip
P. japonica	Candelabra primrose
Rheum palmatum	Chinese rhubarb
Sagittaria japonica	Japanese arrowhead
Trollius europaeus	Globe flower
Typha species	Cattail
Zantedeschia aethiopica *	Calla lily

Tall Backgrounds

*Tender

Botanical name	Common name
Alcea rosea	Hollyhock
Allium giganteum	Decorative onion
Aruncus dioicus	Goatsbeard
Aster novae-angliae	Michaelmas daisy
A. sibiricus	Siberian aster
Astilbe tacquetii superba	False spiraea
Boltonia asteroides	White star
Canna indica and hybrids	Indian canna
Cimicifuga racemosa	Black snakeroot
Dahlia x hybrida	Tuberous dahlia
Delphinium elatum	English delphinium
Digitalis purpurea	English foxglove
Eremurus elwesii	Foxtail lily
Eupatorium fistulosum	Joe-pye weed
Gladiolus x hortulanus	Gladiolus
Helianthus tuberosa	Jerusalem artichoke
Ligularia x przewalskii	Rocket ligularia
Lilium lancifolium	Tiger lily
Macleaya cordata	Plume poppy
Onopordum acanthium	Scotch thistle
Perovskia atriplicifolia	Russian sage
Phlox paniculata	Summer phlox
Verbascum olympicum	Candelabra mullein

Water Plants

*Tender

Botanical name	Common name
Acorus calamus 'Variegatus'	Sweet flag
Arundo donax	Giant reed
Azolla caroliniana	Water fern
Calla palustris	Bog arum
Caltha palustris	Marsh marigold
Cyperus alternifolius *	Umbrella grass
C. papyrus *	Egyptian papyrus
Eichhornia crassipes *	Water hyacinth
Equisetum hyemale	Horsetail
Houttuynia cordata	Chameleon plant
Hydrocleys nymphoides	Water poppy
Iris pseudacorus	Yellow flag iris
I. versicolor	Blue flag iris
Juncus effusus 'Spiralis'	Corkscrew rush
Lobelia cardinalis	Scarlet lobelia, cardinal flower

Botanical name	Common name
Lysichiton americana	Yellow skunk cabbage
Lythrum salicaria	Purple loosestrife
Myosotis scorpioides	Forget-me-not
Myriophyllum aquaticum	Parrot's feather
Nelumbo nucifera	Sacred lotus
Nymphaea hybrids	Waterlily
Orontium aquaticum	Golden club
Pistoia stratiotes *	Water lettuce
Pontederia cordata	Pickerel weed
Sagittaria latifolia	American arrowhead
Spartina pectinata	Prairie cordgrass
Typha species	Cattail
Utricularia vulgaris	Bladderwort

Foliage Effects

In addition to the following specific varieties, consider additional varieties of ornamental grasses, ferns, and hostas for superb foliage effects.

* Tender
† Indicates evergreen perennials

Botanical name	Common name
Acanthus mollis *	Bear's breeches
Aegopodium podagraria	Bishop's weed
Ajuga reptans †	Bugle weed
Alchemilla mollis	Lady's mantle
Artemisia ludoviciana	Wormwood
Arum italicum	Italian arum
Aruncus dioicus	Goatsbeard
Astilbe x *arendsii*	False spiraea
Begonia grandis	Hardy angel's wing begonia
Belchnum occidentale *†	Painted fern
Bergenia cordifolia †	Heart-leaf bergenia
Caltha palustris	Marsh marigold
Canna hortensis *	Indian shot
Centaurea cineraria *	Dusty miller
Cerastium tomentosum	Snow-in-summer
Chrysanthemum ptarmiciflorum *	Dusty miller
Crambe cordifolia *	Sea kale
Cyclamen neapolitanum	Hardy cyclamen
Cyrtomium falcatum *†	Holly fern
Dianthus plumarius †	Cottage pinks
Hedera canarienis *†	Algerian ivy
H. colchica *†	Persian ivy
H. helix †	English ivy
Helleborus niger †	Christmas rose
Hosta 'Frances Williams'	Hosta, Plantain lily
H. sieboldii	Blue hosta

Botanical name	Common name
Juniperus horizontalis †	Creeping juniper
Ligularia x *przewalskii* †	Rocket ligularia
Liriope muscari var. *variegata* †	Variegated lilyturf
Petasites japonica	Butterburr
Stachys byzantina	Lamb's ears
Vinca minor †	Periwinkle
Yucca filamentosa †	Spanish dagger

Slope Cover

*Tender

Botanical name	Common name
Aegopodium podagraria 'Variegatum'	Bishop's weed
Arabis caucasica	Rock cress
Armeria maritima	Thrift
Aubrieta deltoidea	False rock cress
Bougainvillea spectabilis *	Bougainvillea
Carpobrotus edulis *	Hottentot fig
Cerastium tomentosum	Snow-in-summer
Coronaria varia	Crown vetch
Cortaderia selloana *	Pampas plume
Dicentra eximia	Bleeding heart
Drosanthemum floribundum *	Rosy ice plant
Euphorbia epithymoides	Cushion spurge
Festuca ovina var. *glauca*	Blue fescue
Forsythia x *pendula*	Weeping forsythia
Hemerocallis hybrids	Daylily
Hypericum calycinum *	St.-John's-wort
Juniperus horizontalis	Creeping juniper
Lathyrus latifolius	Perennial sweet pea
Lonicera japonica 'Halliana'	Japanese honeysuckle
Pelargonium peltatum	Ivy-leaf geranium
Pennisetum alopecuroides	Fountain grass (also many other drought-tolerant grasses)
Polygonum capitatum *	Knotweed
Rosmarinus officinalis 'Prostratus' *	Creeping rosemary
Santolina virens	Lavender cotton
Sedum kamtschaticum	Yellow sedum
Trachelospermum jasminoides *	Confederate jasmine
Vinca minor	Periwinkle
Yucca filamentosa	Spanish dagger

Climbers

*Tender

Botanical name	Common name
Actinidia kolomikta	Hardy kiwi vine
Akebia quinata	Five-leaf akebia
Allamanda cathartica 'Williamsi' *	Yellow allamanda
Ampelopsis brevipedunculata	Porcelain berry
Aristolochia durior	Dutchman's pipe
Bougainvillea spectablis	Bougainvillea
Campsis radicans	Trumpet creeper
Celastrus orbiculatus	Oriental bittersweet
C. scandens	America bittersweet
Clematis hybrids	Many kinds, such as 'Nelly Moser', 'Jackman's Superb', 'Doctor Ruppell'
C. maximowicziana	Sweet autumn clematis
C. montana 'Rubra'	Montana clematis
Convolvulus mauritanicus *	Perennial morning glory
Euonymus fortunei	Winter creeper
Gelsemium sempervirens *	Carolina jasmine
Hedera helix	English ivy
Hydrangea anomala var. petiolaris	Climbing hydrangea
Jasminum officinale *	White jasmine
Lathyrus latifolius	Perennial sweet pea
Lonicera x heckrotti	Gold-flame honeysuckle
L. japonica 'Halliana'	Japanese honeysuckle
L. sempervirens	Trumpet honeysuckle
Parthenocissus quinquefolia	Virginia creeper
P. tricuspidata	Boston ivy
Passiflora caerulea	Passion vine
Polygonum aubertii	Silverlace vine
Rosa	Climbers of various kinds, such as 'American Pillar', 'Blaze', 'Dortmund', 'Golden Showers', 'New Dawn'
Trachelospermum jasminoides *	Star jasmine
Wisteria floribunda	Japanese wisteria
W. sinensis	Chinese wisteria

Salt Tolerance

*Tender

Botanical name	Common name
Agapanthus africanus *	Lily of the Nile
Agave attenuata *	Mexican century plant
Aloe ferox *	South African aloe
Amaryllis belladonna	Amaryllis
Ammophila arenariaes	European beach grass
A. breviligulata	American beach grass
Arctostaphylos species	Bearberry, manzanita
Arenaria verna	Sandwort
Armeria maritima	Thrift
Artemisia schmidtiana	Sagebrush
A. stellerana	Beach wormwood
Carpobrotus edulis	Hottentot fig
Convolvulus mauritanica *	Perennial morning glory
Crambe cordifolia	Sea kale
Crocosmia x crocosmia	Montbretia
Cytisus species	Broom
Drosanthemum species *	Rosy ice plant
Echeveria elegans *	Mexican snowball
Echinops species	Globe thistle
Erigeron species	Beach aster, fleabane
Eryngium species	Sea holly
Festuca ovina var. glauca	Blue fescue
Gypsophila paniculata	Baby's breath
Hemerocallis species	Daylily
Hydrangea hortensis	Hydrangea
Kniphofia uvaria	Red-hot poker
Lavatera trimestris	Beach mallow
Limonium latifolium	Sea lavender
Nerine bowdenii *	Nerine
Oenothera missouriensis	Evening primrose
Osteospermum fruticosum *	Trailing African daisy
Pelargonium peltatum *	Ivy-leaf geranium
Phormium tenax *	New Zealand flax
Romneya coulteri *	Tree poppy
Salvia leucantha *	Mexican sage
Uniola paniculata	Sea oats
Yucca filamentosa	Spanish dagger
Zantedeschia aethiopica *	Calla lily

Chapter Two

The World of Perennials

hether you have dust-dry desert soil, a water-saturated swamp, or a cliff-top meadow swept with salt spray, there are perennial plants that will make your world more appealing. This chapter concentrates on identifying major perennial groups by two extremely useful common physical qualities (spreading and vining), by the two most common environmental influences on flowering performance (sun and shade), and by major plant classifications (such as perennial bulbs, grasses, and herbs). These plant groups offer so many species and varieties that they are often used by themselves to create a beautiful garden space. Sites with problems caused by environmental influences, such as a wetlands habitat or a coastal location, are covered in Chapter Four, where they are discussed in the context of design.

This chapter begins by presenting a wealth of ideas using true perennials—plants you might find in the "Perennials" section of your local garden center, for example. It presents separately a range of design ideas using perennial bulbs because they can be used exclusively for floral displays, especially in the spring, when tulips and daffodils tend to dominate the home landscape. Also, mail-order companies and garden centers usually offer bulbs in separate catalogs, or in separate departments.

Perennial herbs have a section to themselves because herb gardening has become immensely popular in its own right. In today's health-conscious world, many herbs are grown in specially designed herb gardens for culinary value, particularly as replacement flavoring for salt in many diets. Also, many home gardeners are interested in making herbal handicrafts, such as potpourris, dried arrangements, and herbal wreaths. Since many useful herbs have inconspicuous flowers, making herb gardens decorative takes a special skill, relying more on subtle foliage effects (such as

silvery leaves), a sculptural quality (such as a cushionlike form), and the placement of an attractive garden accent (such as a sundial or a beehive).

When choosing perennial varieties in general, flowering effect alone should not be your only criterion. Take a good look at foliage effects, especially foliage *contrasts* that pair well or create eye-catching triad combinations of leaf color, leaf texture, and especially leaf *shape*. For example, the broad, savoyed, dark green paddle-shaped leaves of many hostas are exquisite when contrasted with the feathery, arching, light green leaves of ostrich fern (*Matteuccia struthiopteris*). Similarly, the heavily indented, spiny, dark green leaves of bear's breeches (*Acanthus mollis*) look sensational beside the slender, arching, straw-colored leaves of fountain grass (*Pennisetum alopecuroides*).

Ornamental grasses are another important plant group, especially for sunny situations and where interesting foliage effects are desired (though many offer the bonus of shade tolerance and magnificent flowers). The term *ornamental grass* is not a clear-cut scientific classification because, botanically, only members of the family Gramineae (such as pampas plume and bamboos) are true grasses, so this book sides with the nursery industry by also including grass impostors, such as sedges, rushes, and lilyturf (*Liriope* species). When you scan the images presented in this section, you may be surprised to discover that grasses are not only green, but also red, blue, yellow, silver, brown, and amber.

When considering plants for sun or shade, you should be able to recognize the different degrees of sunlight and different degrees of shade. In fact, it is not necessarily direct sunlight, but light *intensity*, that affects the flowering performance of a sun-loving plant. For example, the majority of flowering perennials enjoy at least six hours of direct sunlight a day, but sunlight shining on a perennial bed that is backed by a hedge and fronted by a lawn is considerably different from the sunlight that shines on a bed backed by a white stucco wall and fronted by a patio of white landscape chips. A garden designer must realize not only that the two environmental conditions may call for a different plant palette (many pale or pastel colors would bleach out in the latter situation), but also that the reflected sunlight in the latter bed may be too strong and may burn up plants that are sensitive to heat.

Similarly, there are many kinds of shade. Garden lilies, azaleas, and rhododendrons, for example, thrive in diffused sunlight. They love the dappled shade of a high-overhead deciduous tree canopy, but they will flower poorly in dark shade, the kind that exists in a woodland of closely spaced pines. This kind of deep shade may allow only a population of foliage plants to survive, such as ferns, mosses, hostas, periwinkle, and ivy. The scientific world has proved that light is so critical to the growth of plants that one percent more light can produce a 100-percent increase in flowering performance. Therefore, in a problem shade area, the removal of a single overhead tree branch—or the simple act of painting a dark fence white—may be sufficient to make the difference between failure and success. Also, it is not so much the weakened light that many shade-loving plants appreciate, but the cool soil conditions that shade provides. Many perennials famous for shade (including primroses and rhododendrons) will thrive out in the open if the soil is kept cool by a humus-rich soil, a covering of mulch, and plentiful natural rainfall or frequent irrigation. You can also make soil cool by rimming a larger plant with smaller plants. And this brings up the subject of groundcovers.

In the perennial mix there are many plants (commonly called *groundcovers*) that will cover the ground like a carpet. Instead of climbing up to create a curtain of foliage and flowers, they spread out, either by dividing vigorously, seeding prolifically, or sending out runners (long roots or stems that form colonies).

Some groundcover perennials are so aggressive that they will knit together to make a beautiful weed-suffocating barrier. The bronze-leaf form of bugle weed (*Ajuga reptans*) not only is evergreen, but also produces beautiful blue flowers in spring. It spreads by division and by seeding itself. For a stunning color contrast, pair it with the silvery leaves of hardy lamb's ears (*Stachys byzantina*). It, too, spreads by division and reseeds itself. Both will effectively deter weeds.

Some groundcovers are well behaved. For example, both periwinkle and pachysandra are evergreen and good to use in deep shade; they are slow growing and easily confined to specific areas. There also are aggressive groundcovers that can quickly outgrow their bounds and become pests in confined spaces. This is particularly true of many ornamental grasses, such as pampas grass and fountain grass, which may reseed like weeds in parts of the Southwest. However, an aggressive characteristic can be a blessing when large stretches of bare ground need covering, especially for control of soil erosion.

A low groundcover planting may be desirable for many other reasons: to add a decorative edge to perennial beds and borders; to soften expanses of concrete, brick, and flagstone (by having a groundcover creep in from the edges); and to shade the roots of plants, such as clematis and garden lilies, that like their heads in the sun but their roots kept cool.

Many tall perennials, such as garden lilies and delphiniums, also need a low-growing, spreading plant to hide their lower stems, which may be bare of foliage at flowering time. In the case of lilies, a groundcover of ferns and Lenten roses is especially attractive; with delphiniums, which are predominantly blue, consider a pink-flowering shrub rose such as The Fairy.

When you find that a particular flowering groundcover thrives in your location, capitalize on it and consider planting it generously. Some of the examples in this chapter, such as heathers in a woodland clearing and creeping phlox on a sunny slope, offer a range of colors that allows them to be used like a quilt to create a flowering lawn.

When choosing vining plants, be sure to consider *how* they climb. Will they climb unaided (by tendrils or suckers), or will they need a strong trellis for support? Many climbers, such as climbing roses, are really misnamed, since they will rarely climb unless the gardener trains the canes to grow upward by tying them securely to a support. In the wild, clematis usually climbs by weaving its slender stems through a tangle of branches on an adjacent shrub, and even a porous brick wall or a post will not support a clematis vine unaided. In the examples shown in this chapter, and in other parts of the book, you will find some good ideas for arbors and arches.

Consider also the aggressive nature of some vines, such as wisteria and Japanese honeysuckle, which can take a stranglehold on young trees and shrubs, suffocating them. If trained over a flimsy wooden fence, they rot it quickly by trapping moisture, just as English ivy does on barn siding. Metal supports for wisteria make more sense.

Perennial vines can do more than carry color high above the limits of other perennials. They can cover unsightly construction features, such as a monotonous stretch of wall, fence, or chain-link fencing. They can be used like a lace curtain to drape down from a balcony, a roof line, or a strong wire strung high over a garden; especially useful are white-flowering kinds like silverlace vine (*Polygonum aubertii*) and sweet autumn clematis (*Clematis maximowicziana*). Many vines, such as clematis and wisteria, develop sinuous woody trunks that look beautiful when stripped of their lower branches to accentuate their flowing lines, especially when coiling up into a tree canopy. Perhaps the most sophisticated use of vines is the weaving of two different kinds for a beautiful color contrast or color harmony. For example, a yellow-flowering Lady Banks rose among the blue blossoms of a wisteria vine is a feature of many southern gardens in spring.

Also consider the merits of vines noted for beautiful autumn coloration, such as Virginia creeper (*Parthenocissus quinquefolia*). The five-fingered, serrated leaves turn brilliant red and do not damage stonework or fences as does common English ivy. If you want a garden full of hummingbirds, plant the orange-flowered native trumpet creeper (*Campsis radicans*) or its large-flowered hybrid, 'Madame Galen'. This vine grows up to ten feet a year, its leaves resemble those of wisteria, and beautiful trumpet-shaped flowers full of nectar bloom continuously all summer.

"Tapestry plantings" that combine a rich assortment of floral colors, leaf textures, and plant forms create the most dramatic perennial borders. This curving border features towering blue English delphiniums (*Delphinium elatum*), tapering pink and white English foxgloves (*Digitalis purpurea*), bold swaths of foamy, cream-colored goatsbeard (*Aruncus dioicus*), and flat-headed white shasta daisies (*Leucanthemum* x *superbum*), creating a river of gently flowing highs and lows, lights and darks. Evergreen cones in the distance create a bold formal contrast to the colorful flowers. A stone wall, densely covered with lush, deep green ivy, provides a strong, disciplined background for this exuberant planting scheme.

Red, pink, and green make a color harmony that was popular with the Impressionist painters. Here, in Claude Monet's garden, dark crimson perennial hollyhock (*Alcea rosea*) not only carries color high into the sky but is a perfect companion to the tree-form roses—in two tones of pink—seen in the background.

When restoring the garden of a historic property, it's a good idea to use bold clumps of old-fashioned perennials, such as here in the garden of the historic Moffatt Ladd house in Portsmouth, New Hampshire. The conspicuous blue-green seed pods of annual poppies and the decorative green foliage of the later-blooming perennials enhance the brilliant display of rose-pink summer phlox (*Phlox paniculata*) and golden perennial sunflower (*Heliopsis* x *multiflorus*). Both make vigorous clumps in the garden display, and they are excellent for cutting.

▶

The warm, soft color scheme of this perennial bed edging a lawn glows like a summer sunset and is made up of hardy, heat-resistant, summer-flowering perennials. These include cantaloupe-colored daylily Melonade, pink wine cups (*Oenothera speciosa*), rosy-pink *Phlox maculata* 'Alpha', and golden yellow dwarf daylily Stella de Oro, as shown in the display gardens of Spring Hill Nurseries, Tipp City, Ohio.

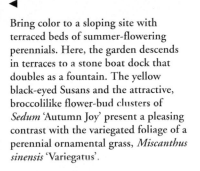

◀

Bring color to a sloping site with terraced beds of summer-flowering perennials. Here, the garden descends in terraces to a stone boat dock that doubles as a fountain. The yellow black-eyed Susans and the attractive, broccolilike flower-bud clusters of *Sedum* 'Autumn Joy' present a pleasing contrast with the variegated foliage of a perennial ornamental grass, *Miscanthus sinensis* 'Variegatus'.

▶

Careful attention to architectural detail can help to integrate a house and garden. The British teak bench in this courtyard garden is painted black to match the black shutters of a nearby cottage. Fall-blooming perennials include several varieties of New England asters, silvery lamb's ears, white pearly everlasting, lavender-blue *Eupatorium coelestinum,* and rusty red *Sedum* 'Autumn Joy'.

◀

Two of the most colorful hardy perennials of late spring are Oriental poppies (*Papaver orientale*) and bearded irises (*Iris* × *germanica*). Here, in Monet's garden at Giverny, France, they make good companions in a mixed perennial bed.

Ornamental grasses are especially beautiful when planted close to water features. Here, autumn-flowering Formosa maiden grass (*Miscanthus transmorriensis*) veils a formal water garden at Wave Hill, New York, with its elegant, arching plumes echoing the colors of the porcupine grass (*Miscanthus sinensis* 'Stricta') at the far end of the pool.

Driveways beg to be edged with perennials to soften their hard lines. This coastal driveway in Carmel, California, features salt-tolerant South African ice plants—red *Lampranthus spectabilis* and white *Osteospermum fruticosum*—plus pastel-pink flower clusters of an Indian hawthorn (*Raphiolepis indica*). The low, prostrate form of blue-flowering California lilac (*Ceanothus*), which is just starting to flower, weaves its lustrous dark green leaves among the perennials.

The conspicuous, feathery flower plumes of false spiraea (*Astilbe* x *arendsii*) are sensational massed beside a waterlily pool. They flower in early summer, just as the hardy waterlilies start to bloom, and their red, pink, and white flower clusters echo the colors of the waterlilies.

The edges of a lawn are perfect places to establish perennial beds. This mixed border of spring-flowering bulbs forms an edging of informal, flowing lines. Each pendant yellow flower cluster of the tall crown imperials (*Fritillaria imperialis* 'Aurea') displays a rakish crown of leaves, echoing the sharply pointed petals of the bicolored lily-flowered Marietta tulips.

Tulips planted alone can look too regimental and show patches of ugly bare soil. Here, low-growing grape hyacinths (*Muscari armeniaca*) weave a ribbon of blue among clumps of peony-flowered tulips. A good rule of thumb when planting tulips in clumps is to use at least fifteen bulbs. Anything less usually gives a sparse appearance.

In warm-climate gardens like this one in San Clemente, California, tender spring-flowering bulbs can provide early spring color. These beds, which follow a narrow path down to the beach, feature yellow, pink, and orange Persian buttercups (*Ranunculus asiaticus*) and blue Dutch irises (*Iris* x *hollandica*) flowering among clumps of perennials that will bloom later in the season.

◀

A sunny slope can be informally planted with early-spring-flowering waterlily tulips (*Tulipa kaufmanniana*) and fragrant Dutch hyacinths. These generally bloom several weeks ahead of the main hybrid tulip displays, about the same time as daffodils.

▲

Mass plantings of Spanish bluebells (*Endymion hispanica*) cover the woodland floor at Winterthur Garden, Delaware. Spanish bluebells are a lighter blue than English bluebells, they have bolder flower spikes, and they are more widely adaptable. Their only drawback is that they lack the fragrance English bluebells are famous for.

◀

Masses of trumpet daffodils declare spring's arrival when naturalized at the edge of a lawn. Notice how the owners have planted the bulbs in distinct color groups, with white in the foreground and yellow behind; they have scattered a few of the yellows among the whites to eliminate any sense of formality.

The owner of this country home has chosen to say "welcome" to visitors by edging the driveway with parallel flower borders of mixed annuals and perennials. The lemon yellow garden lilies in the foreground are hardy summer-flowering perennial bulbs, planted in combination with perennial white yarrow and yellow black-eyed Susans.

Kaffir lilies (*Clivia miniata*) are tender flower bulbs that are popular pot plants for decorating sunrooms and conservatories in the northern states. Where winters are relatively frost-free, as in Southern California and Florida, they are sensational planted in light shade, where they flower in early spring.

Hardy autumn crocuses (*Colchicum autumnale*) bloom at the end of summer, after the straplike leaves have died down. They are particularly beautiful planted at the edge of a woodland and between shrubs along the house foundation. They can also be planted under grass to flower in drifts across a lawn.

A popular summer bulb for shady gardens is the fancy-leaved caladium (*Caladium* x *hortulanum*). It is grown for its colorful foliage, and no two leaves are ever the same. The bulbs are tender and, in areas prone to frost, must be taken up in autumn and stored until spring in a frost-free area. Here, at the Missouri Botanical Garden, pink and white varieties create a beautiful color harmony with pink verbenas.

Elegant ostrich ferns (*Matteuccia pensylvanica*), native to the Eastern Seaboard, edge a stepping-stone path and help to establish a wild, informal look at a formal entrance. They are shown here in company with the heart-shaped leaves of hostas, clumps of spent daffodil foliage, an evergreen boxwood, and evergreen cypress.

Though most ferns are shades of green, a few are golden or silvery. Here, the silvery fronds of a Japanese painted fern (*Athyrium goeringianum* 'Pictum') spill onto a flight of steps, helping to soften the hard lines of flagstone. Though hardy, these ferns are decid-uous, going dormant in winter.

A fern-fringed path is a particularly appealing feature of woodland gardens. Here, at Bok Tower Gardens in Florida, a meandering rustic path, covered with shredded dried leaves, is edged along its entire length with tender sword ferns (*Nephrolepis cordifolia*). Gardeners in the northern states can achieve a similar effect with the evergreen Christmas fern (*Polystichum acrostichoides*).

▶

In states with mild winters, groves of sago palms (*Cycas revoluta*) resemble masses of tree ferns. Here, at Lotusland garden, Santa Barbara, California, they occupy an entire hillside in a part of the garden landscaped to look like Japan. The mosslike groundcover is baby's tears (*Soleirolia soleirolii*), a tender perennial.

▲

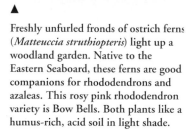

Freshly unfurled fronds of ostrich ferns (*Matteuccia struthiopteris*) light up a woodland garden. Native to the Eastern Seaboard, these ferns are good companions for rhododendrons and azaleas. This rosy pink rhododendron variety is Bow Bells. Both plants like a humus-rich, acid soil in light shade.

▲

The maidenhair fern (*Adiantum pedatum*) has an old-fashioned appeal that is perfectly suited to Colonial-style cottage gardens like this one. It forms billowing clumps of delicate compound leaves. A deciduous plant, it turns brown and dies back to its roots after frost.

▶

Ornamental grasses make especially welcome contributions to the garden in autumn. This garden shows a good cross section of autumn colors, including creamy-colored ribbon grass (*Phalaris arundinaria*) in the foreground, red blood grass (*Imperata cylindrica*) at the right, green eulalia grass (*Miscanthus*) at the left, brown-tufted hair grass (*Deschampsia*) and amber feather reed grass (*Calamagrostis*) at the rear, and blue-green giant reed (*Arundo donax*) in the far background.

▶

Ornamental grasses combine beautifully with late-blooming perennials. A mistlike mass of dropseed grass (*Sporobolus*) contrasts with the white feathertop (*Pennisetum villosum*), black fountain grass (*Pennisetum alopecuroides*), and pampas plume (*Cortaderia*) at the rear and the amber fountain grass at the right. Two kinds of sedum, rusty red Autumn Joy and pink Brilliancy, are hardy autumn-flowering perennials.

◀

Use foliage contrasts to create artistic displays with easy-to-care-for ornamental grasses. Here, the leaf blades of amber-colored feather reed grass (*Calamagrostis acutiflora* 'Stricta') combine elegantly with blue-green giant Chinese silver grass (*Miscanthus*), bronze fountain grass, and variegated sweet flag. The slender leaves of the grasses contrast well with the broad, mottled, paddle-shaped leaves of a banana plant and the red canna blossoms in the background.

Use bold clumps of drought-tolerant ornamental grasses for slopes. In the Hillside Garden at Wave Hill, New York, ornamental grasses rub shoulders with annuals and perennials in an artistic arrangement of subtle autumn hues, produced mostly by foliage. Crowning the slope is an explosion of *Miscanthus sinensis* 'Silver Feather' and a cascade of silvery white *Miscanthus sinensis* 'Variegata'. Slender leaf blades of fountain grass and towering stems of giant reed (*Arundo donax*) add dramatic foliage effects. Palm yucca (*Yucca pendule*) stabs the sky with broad, pointed blue-green leaves. Pink Fairy rose and orange *Zinnia angustifolia* (an annual) add splashes of floral color.

A magnificent specimen of dwarf fountain grass (*Pennisetum alopecuroides* 'Hamlyn') erupts with soft pink flower spikes in a drought-tolerant California garden planted mostly with cacti and succulents. Soft light from a setting autumn sun backlights the feathery grass plumes, making them shine with a brilliance that contrasts well with the stiff forms of agaves, yuccas, aloes, and prickly pear cacti.

Ornamental grasses are a beautiful way to line a driveway and also a brick walk leading to the front entrance of a house. The elegant, cascading amber flower spikes of *Miscanthus transmorriensis* (a tender perennial) are bathed in sunlight. In the shade of a porch are clumps of hardy black fountain grass (*Pennisetum alopecuroides* 'Moudry').

The softly swaying leaves of ornamental grasses help to create a naturalistic appearance around an informal swimming pool at the Maryland home of ornamental grass expert Kurt Bluemel. The featured grasses include varieties of eulalia (*Miscanthus sinensis*) and fountain grass (*Pennisetum alopecuroides*). Planting the grasses among boulders simulates a rocky, grassland environment.

This sterile form of dwarf pampas plume (*Cortaderia selloana* 'Pumila') is compact enough to grow in a tub. In this photograph, early morning light illuminates the brilliance of its silky white flower plumes.

Replacing part of a lawn with ornamental grasses cuts down on maintenance chores. The owner of this house has replaced a rectangle of lawn with semicircular terraced beds that are lined with boulders and hold a collection of ornamental grasses. Space between the grasses is kept weed-free by a mulch of shredded pine bark. Flowering in autumn is *Miscanthus sinensis* 'Gracillimus'.

Ornamental grasses make excellent pot plants for decorating decks and patios. Here, the soft, mounded form of hardy *Hakonechloa macrantha*, in autumn coloring, contrasts well with the spiky leaves of a tender dragon palm (*Dracaena* species) in the perennial garden at Wave Hill, New York.

This collection of sun-loving hardy perennials and annuals is particularly well suited to growing conditions in the Midwest. The bright, hot colors of yellow perennial coreopsis, purple loosestrife, pink coneflower, annual yellow gloriosa daisies, and burgundy petunias are accentuated by a tall evergreen windbreak.

This redwood moongate is designed with a porthole and wide-set slats that create a frame through which approaching visitors can view a beautiful garden of perennials and annuals. This style of gate is much more inviting than solid gates, which allow no view of the garden beyond.

Courtyard gardens provide good shelter for perennials, especially in coastal locations. This courtyard, at historic Carmel Mission in California, is a haven for perennials popular on the West Coast. Along the overhang of a cloister, a wisteria vine drapes clusters of blue flowers, while along the wall, perennial valerian flaunts bright red flowers. Because of the sandy soil, almost all the flower beds are raised. They are lined with boulders and filled with compost.

Steep hillsides sometimes need landscaping with large boulders and retaining walls to hold pockets of soil in which perennials will take hold, as in this Vail, Colorado, garden. In spring, the garden sparkles with the iridescent petals of yellow, orange, and red Iceland poppies, cushions of blue forget-me-nots, white perennial candytuft, and dwarf blue bearded irises—all planted along a cascading stream.

Violet and white make an attractive color harmony for spring. This sunny slope produces a bold mass of color using the violet-blue flowers of false rock cress (*Aubrieta deltoidea*), balanced by an equal amount of white from perennial candytuft (*Iberis sempervirens*). Smaller plantings of red tulips and yellow violas add dramatic color contrasts.

A distinctive silvery edging of *Artemisia* 'Silver Brocade' gives a touch of class to a sunny border of rather common summer-flowering perennials. The yellow daylily in this garden, Stella de Oro, is everblooming. If faded flowers are removed, it will bloom nonstop from June until autumn frost.

In areas with mild winters, tender kinds of sedums and century plants can add attractive shapes and subtle colors to rock gardens. Here, rosettes of aquamarine *Echeveria elegans* and a clump of steel blue mescal (*Agave parryi*) complement each other in a bed of mostly succulents, where white annual alyssum and white perennial marguerite daisies help to brighten the display.

▶

Hardy perennial mountain pinks (*Phlox subulata*) thrive on sunny slopes, creating what appears to be a flowering lawn in spring. The colors include white, pink, red, and shades of blue. After flowering, the plants maintain a tight mat of silvery gray evergreen leaves. Taller wild blue phlox (*Phlox divaricata*) forms a flowering hedge across the top of the slope.

▼

Careful plant choices can produce a perennial garden that is still vibrant with color in midsummer after months of drought. Two good plants are seen in this California garden. In the center, the silvery, sinuous flower spikes of biennial *Verbascum olympicum* create a sculptural accent. Flowering with wild abandon in the background is a mass of glittering pink perennial wine cups (*Oenothera speciosa*).

◀

Where gardeners in cold-winter states might use mountain pinks as a flowering perennial groundcover, gardeners in mild-winter states, such as coastal California, can use tender African ice plants. Highly salt-tolerant and drought-resistant, magenta-colored *Lampranthus spectabilis* covers a sandy cliff-top site overlooking the Pacific Ocean at Carmel, California.

Here are two good plants for humus-rich, acid soil that deserve to be more widely grown. Clumps of evergreen hardy perennial Lenten roses (*Helleborus orientalis*) surround a clump of evergreen dwarf box huckleberry (*Gaylussacia brachycera*) along a shaded woodland path. The pink bell-shaped flowers of the huckleberry produce small, edible, blueberrylike fruits in late summer. Both these plants are very compatible with rhododendrons.

Many shady woodland areas have boggy soil. An abundance of moss, seen here on the right, is a good indicator of a moisture-saturated soil. Both the blue forget-me-nots and the pink Japanese primulas thrive in a water-saturated environment, and will even reseed themselves to form large colonies.

Many kinds of spring-flowering bulbs, such as the crown imperials, daffodils, and tulips in this woodland garden, will last longer in lightly shaded areas because they enjoy cool conditions. To bloom like this, spring-flowering bulbs must be planted in early autumn in humus-rich, fertile soil with good drainage.

◀

If you have an unused structure on your property, you might be able to build a garden around it. Many older properties still feature springhouses—stone buildings that served as a primitive form of refrigeration in Colonial days. Using the building as a decorative accent, the owner here has surrounded it with azaleas and has lined the stream with drifts of handsome ostrich ferns. A small arched footbridge spans a spillway that forms a pond.

▶

To gain fall color, consider arching paths with the branches of an ornamental crabapple, such as *Malus floribunda*, here bright with scarlet-red fruits. The vaulting branches form a leafy tunnel that helps to frame a clump of lavender-blue hosta flowers. The bright green fronds of a cinnamon fern arch into the path from a raised bed created with boulders that are hidden by evergreens.

◀

To create a shade garden under a high tree canopy, the owners of this woodland garden took inspiration from Japanese garden design and created a moss garden, using perennial evergreen mosses they found growing naturally. To be kept weed-free, moss needs a highly acid soil, rigorous weeding throughout the year, and watering during dry spells. It is by no means maintenance-free.

Hardy perennial hostas are one of the best groundcovers for damp, shady areas. The large, heart-shaped leaves often exhibit attractive variegation patterns, and most of them produce beautiful bell-shaped flowers held well above the foliage. This variety, Francee, displays heavily savoyed leaves with a bicolored blue-and-chartreuse pattern.

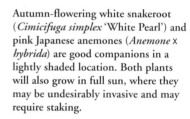

Autumn-flowering white snakeroot (*Cimicifuga simplex* 'White Pearl') and pink Japanese anemones (*Anemone* x *hybrida*) are good companions in a lightly shaded location. Both plants will also grow in full sun, where they may be undesirably invasive and may require staking.

Hybrids of the heart-leaf bergenia (*Bergenia cordifolia*) make attractive evergreen groundcovers for light shade. They tolerate dry or moist soil and are suitable for edging large perennial beds and borders. The lustrous, leathery, green cabbage-size leaves often turn burnished bronze and red in winter and look especially good planted along stream banks and spilling over flagstone paving.

Though individually the two-tone, red-and-yellow pendant flowers of wild columbine (*Aquilegia canadensis*) are small, healthy clumps produce myriad sparkling blossoms that will brighten up a lightly shaded space in early spring. Supporting them in this Connecticut woodland garden are clumps of blue bugle weed, blue phlox, and the young leaves of a variegated hosta.

Many perennials offer colorful leaves in addition to interesting flowers, such as the hardy perennial plume poppy (*Macleaya cordata*), with its deeply lobed, blue-green leaves and feathery, buff-colored flower plumes. Here, it stands out among other subtle foliage contrasts on a verdant slope.

A leafy tapestry of green hues and appealing shapes decorates and softens the edges of a formal pool. Perennials and small shrubs grace the perimeter of this pool. Prominent is a fig (*Ficus edulis*) growing in a submerged pot that is taken indoors during winter. Cushion-shaped mugho pines, a creeping euonymus, and gray-green lavender complete the picture.

Tender baby's tears (*Soleirolia soleirolii*) is a good substitute for moss outdoors in a sheltered, lightly shaded, frost-free garden space, or under glass. In addition to rimming ornamental pools, it is suitable for planting between broken flagstone and stepping stones to cover bare soil, though it will not tolerate heavy foot traffic.

Hostas are among the best plants for shade; they have dozens of uses, and there are hundreds of varieties to choose from, some with fragrant flowers. Here, they line a woodland path leading to a tool shed. Blue-green and bicolored varieties are grouped in the foreground; solid colors, arranged by height and leaf size, extend all the way to the shed door. All hostas prefer a cool, moist location.

The fine, tousled foliage of ornamental grasses can help to soften the stiff, regimented forms of conifers. This landscaped swimming pool relies heavily on evergreen conifers for ornamental effect, but it includes a few strategically placed perennial grasses close to the pool edge. They include clumps of cream-colored variegated mondo grass (center) and blue fescue (left).

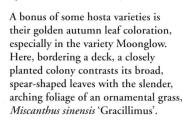

A bonus of some hosta varieties is their golden autumn leaf coloration, especially in the variety Moonglow. Here, bordering a deck, a closely planted colony contrasts its broad, spear-shaped leaves with the slender, arching foliage of an ornamental grass, *Miscanthus sinensis* 'Gracillimus'.

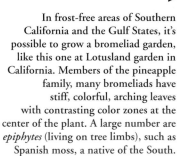

A foliage composition may be surprisingly vibrant. Here, a cluster of tender perennials with exotic leaf shapes and colors helps to decorate the base of a column that supports an arbor. Spotted maple leaf *Abutilon pictum* (right) is sandwiched between a plain green *Abutilon hybridum* (left) and a begonialike *Acalypha wilkesiana* 'Hoffmanii' (right). Variegated geranium and annual sweet alyssum add touches of cream and white to the arrangement.

In frost-free areas of Southern California and the Gulf States, it's possible to grow a bromeliad garden, like this one at Lotusland garden in California. Members of the pineapple family, many bromeliads have stiff, colorful, arching leaves with contrasting color zones at the center of the plant. A large number are *epiphytes* (living on tree limbs), such as Spanish moss, a native of the South.

▲

In a charming small-space herb garden, this simple design uses a birdbath as a focal point in the middle of a square bed; stepping stones from one side lead to the birdbath. A hedge of perennial raspberry canes separates the herb garden from a vegetable garden. Crimson nasturtiums and scarlet Shirley poppies add splashes of floral color among leafy clumps of silvery lady's mantle and lime green lovage.

◄

Wattle fences, made of woven branches, were popular in monastery gardens and lend an old-fashioned charm to a contemporary herb garden. In this herb garden, low wattle fences define quadrants, four beds of equal size that meet in the middle at a beehive. Stepping stones, strategically placed inside the beds, allow easy access for harvesting the mostly culinary herbs.

Many herbs are attractive enough to grow right alongside ornamentals. This formal perennial garden features an assortment of herbs planted in pots and mixed in beds with ornamental perennials and flowering shrubs. The rustic arbor in the background doubles as a garden seat.

Container plantings can be enlivened by a mix of flowering plants and herbs. A flowering mandevilla vine and silvery dusty miller are common container subjects, but they play only a supporting role in this imaginative composition, where lemon grass takes center stage. Prostrate rosemary and a purple-leaf basil complete the composition.

In hot climates, lath houses create a more hospitable environment for perennial plants. At the Sherman Library in Newport Beach, California, this lath house has wide, slatted shelves that display an assortment of perennial herbs in decorative terra-cotta containers. The lower shelf contains society garlic, salad burnet, parsley, and ginger. The top shelf features thyme, sorrel, and comfrey.

The reflective surfaces of stucco walls help to provide sufficient light to grow herbs in shady areas. This heavily shaded courtyard at the historic Virginia Robinson Garden in Beverly Hills, California, features a large collection of mostly culinary herbs in terra-cotta pots, with stone cherubs as decorative accents.

Clematis is considered the queen of vines, an excellent choice for covering a bare utility pole and also walls and fences. The vines themselves are light and airy and do not rot wood as easily as more aggressive stranglers like wisteria and climbing hydrangea. This variety, Henryi, is an extremely free-flowering white that blooms in early summer.

Scarlet trumpet honeysuckle (*Lonicera sempervirens*) is a hardy, easy-to-grow flowering vine native to the Eastern Seaboard, from Massachussetts to Florida. There is also a less common yellow-flowering form. Here, at Colonial Williamsburg, it pushes its long, slender, arching canes through an old-fashioned picket fence.

A French nurseryman crossed the hardy native American trumpet creeper (*Campsis radicans*) with a tender Chinese species (*Campsis grandiflora*) and produced this extremely free-flowering, large-flowered hardy hybrid called Madame Galen. Attractive to hummingbirds, and capable of growing ten feet in a season, Madame Galen flowers the second season from a planting of rooted cuttings.

There are varieties of clematis that bloom in different seasons. The native American sweet autumn clematis (*Clematis maximowicziana*) is highly fragrant and blooms in late summer and early autumn. It is invaluable for training along the tops of fences and walls to add a "lace curtain" effect to the landscape.

▲

The Japanese wisteria (*Wisteria floribunda*), in shades of blue or white, makes one of the best arbor plants for spring flowering. Growing up to 6 feet a year, it needs heavy pruning to be kept within bounds, but the pendulous, glimmering flower clusters may reach several feet in length, as they do here at the Bishop's Close Garden, Portland, Oregon.

▲

Careful training can create a dramatic floral pattern of climbing roses. In this rose garden, climbers are trained over metal frames. The varieties include red Dortmund on the first arch and a darker red, Doctor Huey, on the second arch. Every autumn, each plant is pruned to four main canes, which are tied securely to the frame to prevent damage by winter wind.

◄

Climbing roses are perfect for decorating arbors. The old garden rose Seven Sisters adds an old-fashioned look to this Victorian-style arbor that connects an herb garden and a perennial garden at the historic Moffat-Ladd House, Portsmouth, New Hampshire. Seven Sisters is appropriately named, for it displays its bicolored flowers mostly in clusters of seven.

The most common reason for planting a groundcover is to hide sections of bare soil between a path and ornamental plantings. Here, in a Japanese-style garden, ever-green perennial Japanese spurge (*Pachysandra terminalis*) is planted thickly between azaleas that have been sheared to create soothing mounds, like cushions of moss.

Not only does bugle weed (*Ajuga reptans*) cover the ground with a tight knit of attractive, lustrous green rosettes, but in early spring, its flowers create a carpet of blue. In addition to plain green, there is a bronze-leaf form, as well as a tricolor variety with cream and pink in its leaf coloration, but none are as free-flowering as the variety Blue Bugle, seen here.

In sheltered, frost-free areas, such as Southern California and the Gulf States, tender baby's tears (*Soleirolia soleirolii*) will colonize the bare soil between flagstones and stepping stones. The plants must be pruned frequently to maintain a separation between the colonies and to hold to the outline of the stones of this patio; otherwise, they will quickly weave to-gether to cover the stones completely.

In an acid, humus-rich soil, Scottish heather (*Erica carnea*) can make a spectacular quilt effect, with its mounds of bell-shaped pink, red, and white flowers. Here, in early spring, a mass of deep pink heather is allowed to trail off into white, melting with the white blossoms of a flowering crabapple and two flowering sarvis trees (*Amelanchier* species) in the background.

One of the finest hardy perennials for edging beds is silvery lamb's ears (*Stachys byzantina*), here creating a subtle transition between the brick coping of a swimming pool and a perennial border. A sterile variety, Silver Carpet, produces no flower spikes and hugs the ground more closely than the species. A large-leaf variety, Wave Hill, rarely flowers.

Snow-in-summer is an evergreen hardy perennial with silvery foliage that remains decorative all year. In spring, the low, spreading plants produce masses of snowy white star-shaped flowers. Suitable for planting on dry slopes and for edging paths, they contrast well with bold, spiky dark green leaves such as those of perennial yuccas, seen here.

If your lawn requires too much time to maintain, seek out alternatives. The owner of this small cottage garden along the California coast gave up trying to maintain a picture-perfect lawn and planted a no-mow "flowering lawn" instead, using a mass of trailing, tender perennial African daisies (*Osteospermum fruticosum*). The bristly red flowers of a tender bottlebrush shrub bloom next to the house foundation.

Coastal gardens relatively free of frost can host massive sweeps of rosy ice plant (*Drosanthemum roseum*), flowering mostly in early spring. Its shimmering pink blossoms open only between 10 A.M. and 4 P.M., but they almost completely hide the foliage. At Pebble Beach, California, acres of coastline are planted with this drought-resistant South African perennial.

◄ A combination of needle-leaf evergreens and broad-leaf evergreen shrubs makes an elegant understory planting. In spring in this garden, the lustrous, dark green spear-shaped leaves of a flowering rhododendron, as well as a mounded Japanese andromeda, contrast with the pyramid shapes of conifers outlined against a glittering canopy of pink and white dogwood blossoms.

► Here is a lovely combination for early spring. The March Walk at Winterthur Garden, Delaware, features a mixture of hardy perennial Lenten roses (*Helleborus orientalis*) beneath the arching branches of a pink-flowering *Rhododendron mucronulatum* and a yellow wintersweet (*Chimonanthus praecox*). The purple blossoms of some of the Lenten roses repeat the color of the rhododendron to tie this distinctive companion planting together.

► An attractive combination of woody flowering plants for an early spring display combines yellow *Forsythia* x *intermedia* with scarlet quince (*Chaenomeles speciosa*) and white star magnolia (*Magnolia stellata*)

A favorite place for small shrubs is along the house foundation. A pleasant change from the uninspired "meatballs" of yew and boxwood is an informal placement of peegee hydrangea (*Hydrangea paniculata* 'Grandiflora') interplanted with tuberous dahlias. Flowering in early autumn, they add a distinctive charm to this weekend Tudor-style cottage along the Maine coast.

A garden's reputation can be made exclusively by the use of varieties of rhododendrons. At the start of this grassy woodland walk, a clump of pink-flowering *Rhododendron* 'Roseum Elegans' contrasts with the elegant bronze leaves of a Japanese maple. All the other floral colors along the path are produced by varieties of azalea (which belong to the same botanical family as rhododendrons).

Chinese witch hazels (*Hamamelis mollis*) are an end-of-winter treat, the earliest of all flowering shrubs to bloom in cold-winter areas. The fragrant, spidery flowers appear on leafless branches and look especially beautiful highlighted against a background of evergreens, such as this white pine. The variety Diana (seen here) is the best of the orange-flowered varieties; Arnold's Promise is the best yellow.

A collection of dwarf evergreens contrasts shapes, leaf textures, and dark foliage tones with the bright, ephemeral red and orange autumnal hues of deciduous Japanese maples. The evergreens include a fountain-like *Leucothoe fontanesiana*, a cone-shaped Alberta spruce, and a prostrate *Juniperus chinensis* var. *procumbens*, which drapes its mass of blue-green needles over a retaining wall like a lava flow.

Chapter Three

Regional Differences

The U.S. Department of Agriculture (USDA) has defined ten zones of plant hardiness for North America based on average low winter temperatures; Zone 1 represents the coldest Arctic region, too cold for any type of gardening, and Zone 10 represents the Florida Keys, where frost is virtually unknown and where many tropical plants thrive. The best zones for growing hardy perennials are 4 (the Great Lakes) through 8 (including the Pacific Northwest and the mid-South), since winters between these zones are sufficiently sharp to produce the dormant period that most hardy perennials relish. In Zones 9 and 10, where winter freezing is mild or infrequent (such as in southern coastal California and the Gulf states), many tender perennials can be grown (including exotic desert cacti, bromeliads, and tropical flowering vines).

When choosing perennials for your region, it's important to know their hardiness rating and whether the plants flower in the cool season or the warm season. Many cool-season perennials will flower spectacularly during the spring and autumn months.

Hardy perennials, which tend to be most desirable for garden display, need a sharp, prolonged cold spell during winter. A rest period, or dormancy (induced by chilling), is an essential part of their growth cycle. Lack of cold is the reason many hardy perennials do not do well in parts of Southern California, the Southwest, and the Deep South. However, where it's impossible to grow a particular hardy perennial, such as garden lilies, a tender substitute is usually available.

Even perennials from alpine regions may not do well over most parts of North America, because the winters are too severe. In their native habit, many alpine plants are accustomed to snow cover during winter, which keeps them protected from severe freezing. For this reason, many exotic Himalayan plants, especially species of lilies and primulas, will not survive winters over many parts of North America. Winter snowfall is either unreliable or insufficient to keep the ground covered during the coldest months, and so the plants freeze.

Whether a perennial will survive from year to year in a particular region is influenced not only by winter cold, but also by its exposure to drying winds, by the pattern of rainfall, by heat stress during summer, and by depredation by insect pests or disease. By splitting North America into six broad sections it's possible to discuss some specific regional differences.

The Northeast

The Northeast includes all the New England states, Pennsylvania, New York, and New Jersey. It is a superb growing area for hardy perennials, the inhabited area falling mostly in Zones 5 and 6 on the USDA zone map. The Northeast has four distinct seasons: cold winters, when the ground may freeze solid a foot deep or more; warm, sunny summers combined with high humidity; a cool spring, when the leaves of deciduous trees unfurl; and a cool autumn, when many plants turn beautiful russet colors.

Rainfall in the Northeast is fairly evenly distributed thoughout the year; in summer it comes mostly from heavy downpours caused by thunderstorms, so that gardens may experience long periods of little or no rainfall. Supplemental irrigation during summer may be essential to maintain a healthy perennial garden.

The natural soil is almost entirely acid, so a soil test is advisable to determine if liming is necessary.

Southern California

Gardening in Southern California has undergone a revolution in recent years as growers and landscape architects have weaned property owners away from the difficult-to-emulate English cottage garden and the pseudo-Japanese garden style, and have promoted gardens that use drought-tolerant plants (particularly California natives), succulents, and ornamental grasses. Modern designs are more apt to seek inspiration from Spanish haciendas and missions.

The one European influence that remains strong is the rose garden. However, instead of the disease-susceptible varieties of spindly hybrid teas, many gardeners make use of bushy, antique roses and vigorous climbers.

Another important consideration for drought-prone properties is fire resistance. Tinder-dry, highly inflammable chapparal plants often surround suburban lots, and unless the garden space around the home is devoted to plants that resist flame, there is a high risk of the home's being destroyed. The risk is so great that local county agents now provide lists of plants with good fire resistance.

In California, the most populated areas are along the coast, where the Sierras, a mountain range paralleling the Pacific Ocean, trap cool ocean air. Soils may be highly alkaline and rains infrequent. Space is at a premium, and gardens tend to be small, used mostly as outdoor living spaces because of the pleasantness of the climate year-round. But gardeners are often restricted by steep slopes, where terracing and raised beds are needed to retain good topsoil. Most of coastal California is an ideal growing environment for a vast range of perennials, including many tender varieties. Though frosts are likely in most winters, they are generally mild, and many of the tender perennials, will quickly revive if nipped by frost.

The South

Except in some high-elevation areas, such as the Ozarks and the Blue Ridge Mountains, the South experiences savagely hot summers with high humidity, and mild winters. The southern Atlantic and Gulf coasts usually experience only mild frosts, and south of Vero Beach, Florida, frosts are infrequent.

Because of the high heat and humidity in summer, perennial gardening is mostly confined to lightly shaded areas, especially under the spreading branches of live oaks, with their massive, sinuous limbs and small oval leaves. The soils tend to be sandy or clay, and the addition of loads of humus is generally needed for growing perennials. Few southern gardens are without a planting of the Indian, or Southern, azalea (*Rhododendron indicum*), in combination with white- or pink-flowering native dogwoods (*Cornus florida*). The most sophisticated gardens also use some of the highly fragrant, native deciduous azaleas, such as *Rhododendron austrinum*.

The Pacific Northwest

The climate of the coastal areas of northern California, Oregon, and Washington is, in the United States, closest to an English climate, with mild winters and plentiful rainfall, especially during spring and autumn. The soil tends to be acid, and cool nights throughout most of the year allow some temperamental perennials to be grown with ease. In fact, gardeners in the Pacific Northwest are able to grow more perennial varieties than gardeners in any other part of North America, and parts of this region are famous for the production of tulips, daffodils, dahlias, and garden lilies, among other notable perennial families. Also, perennials grown as annuals on other parts of the continent (such as Iceland poppies, carnations, and four o'clocks) will overwinter in the Pacific Northwest and will bloom again. The area is famous for its displays of summer-flowering perennial bulbs, especially tuberous dahlias, tuberous begonias, and gladiolus. Rich in evergreens, most perennial gardens include dwarf needle evergreens as accents. A skillful blending of foliage of different hues, including silver, blue, yellow, and lime green, mixes well with the more vibrant hues of perennial flowers.

English-style cottage gardens look sensational in most parts of the Pacific Northwest, and so do Japanese-style gardens. Rhododendrons, heather, and camellias excel throughout the Pacific Northwest, particularly the fragrant Mollis and Exbury hybrid rhododendrons (also known as *azaleas*), which tend to be short-lived elsewhere in North America. Roses, too, grow spectacularly.

The Midwest

The Midwest's huge landmass of relatively flat grassland prairie can be defined as everything that lies between the Rocky Mountains in the West and the Allegheny Mountains in the East. It consists largely of desolate, treeless plains; much of it still has remnants of the grassland prairie once browsed by buffalo, with mostly willows and poplar trees concentrated along rivers and creeks. Hot, humid summers and freezing, windswept winters characterize the midwestern states, where the irrigation water sometimes requires amendment because of its alkalinity. Shelter belts around properties are generally the first priority for the success of any perennial garden. Usually, these double-layered windbreaks are made by planting a tough, wind-tolerant evergreen, such as a tall, fast-growing white pine, to take the brunt of the wind, and then a bushy, wind-tolerant deciduous tree, such as a Russian olive, to further dissipate the wind.

Many suburban homes feature a U-shaped design, with the inside of the U forming a sheltered courtyard suitable for growing flowering perennials. In exposed locations, ornamental grasses are popular and are often interplanted with perennials native to the prairie. In shady places, hostas are used extensively for groundcover effect.

The Southwest

The term *xeriscaping* was coined in the Southwest to mean the art of landscape planting for moisture conservation. Xeriscaping not only involves the use of "hardscape" (paving, patios, and decks) but also relies on desert species such as cacti and succulents.

Southwestern soils can be the worst to garden in. Usually, the heavy alkalinity of the topsoil and the concretelike nature of the subsoil (called *caliche*) mean that special planting beds with good topsoil, bounded by brick, landscape ties, or boulders, must be created above the indigenous soil. Where wells may run dry or city water may be rationed, ingenious methods must be considered for storing precious rainfall. These include using sloping surfaces, such as roofs, to form catchments that channel water into cisterns.

Most good perennial gardens in the Southwest are concentrated in light shade that breaks the stressful heat of the sun, particularly by the use of the indigenous mesquite and palo verde trees. Many gardeners also time plantings so that blooming occurs in early spring, when conditions are sufficiently cool to allow spectacular flowering by ice plants, such as the *Lampranthus* species, and tender flowering bulbs, such as Persian buttercups (*Ranunculus asiaticus*).

▶

If you are in search of a hardy, adaptable perennial, try Lenten rose (*Helleborus orientalis*), which is among the hardiest. Blooming in March in the northern states (earlier in the South), Lenten rose thrives in the light shade of winter-flowering shrubs such as witch hazel, or under small trees with decorative bark like the paperbark maple (*Acer griseum*) seen here.

◀

For maximum hardiness, consider old garden varieties, especially among roses and hydrangeas. In autumn, prune climbing roses to four strong canes, and either lay these on the ground, covered with leaves, or tie them firmly to a support. Hydrangeas can be pruned close to the ground each year and the stumps covered with leaves; the plants will sprout new growth in spring.

▲

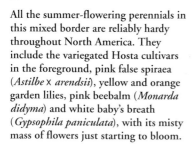

All the summer-flowering perennials in this mixed border are reliably hardy throughout North America. They include the variegated Hosta cultivars in the foreground, pink false spiraea (*Astilbe* x *arendsii*), yellow and orange garden lilies, pink beebalm (*Monarda didyma*) and white baby's breath (*Gypsophila paniculata*), with its misty mass of flowers just starting to bloom.

▶

If you like summer phlox (*Phlox paniculata*) but find it difficult to grow, try planting *Phlox maculata* instead. Like summer phlox, it is hardy into Canada, but it blooms earlier (by as much as three weeks), does not grow as tall, and it is less susceptible to mildew disease. This rose-pink variety, Alpha, is outstanding.

Use hardy, heat-tolerant perennials for an easy-care summer garden. Surrounding this flagstone patio are bicolored daylilies, white shasta daisies, and yellow Moonbeam coreopsis (behind the lounge chair). The yellow daisies are hardy annual gloriosa daisies, bred from the wild black-eyed Susan (*Rudbeckia hirta*). Both the single-flowered (foreground) and the double types (rear) will reseed.

Edge a sunny path with English lavender (*Lavandula angustifolia*) for both color and fragrance. Munstead, the hardiest variety, is shown here edging a flagstone path; Hidcote is a deeper violet-blue color. Lavender needs well-drained soil but will not survive severe winters. To keep old plants decorative, trim them to a tidy mounded shape after frost.

The wall of a house can provide extra protection for perennial plants in places where weather is severe. In this mixed border with annual cosmos and gloriosa daisies, yellow swamp sunflower (*Helianthus* × *multiflorus*) and variegated ribbon grass (*Phalaris arundinacea* 'Picta') enjoy the benefit of a sheltered site.

Two of the hardiest perennials for northern gardens are bicolored blanket flower (*Gaillardia* × *grandiflora*) and yellow dog fennel (*Anthemis sancti-johannis*). They require no special winter protection over most parts of North America. In this garden, they surround miniature roses, which are only moderately hardy and benefit from a covering of shredded leaves to help them through severe winters.

▼

The scarlet flowers and distinctive bronze foliage of summer- and autumn-flowering *Dahlia* 'Bishop of Llandaff' provide a strong color accent in a bed or border of annuals and hardy perennials like the one seen here. The tuberous roots are too tender to overwinter; dig them up each autumn and store them in a frost-free location for replanting after frost danger is past in spring.

▶

Tender perennial *Canna* can dress up otherwise ordinary beds of annuals. The bananalike leaves add a tropical look, and the flower spikes last all summer. This tall red variety is The President. Cannas grow from bulbs. After frost ends the flowering display, dig up the bulbs, clean them of soil, and store them over winter in a frost-free place.

◀

Many tender perennial vines grow fast enough to cover an arbor by the end of the first summer. Here, *Mandevilla* x *amabilis* 'Alice du Pont' flaunts its exotic pink flowers. Mandevilla is too tender to winter outdoors anywhere in the United States except in Florida and Southern California, but northern gardeners can grow them in large containers and move them indoors to a sunny location over winter.

▶

The yellow hibiscuslike flowers of *Allamanda cathartica* appear continuously all summer until fall frost. The vine is fast growing and easily cultivated in large pots. Though it needs a frost-free climate to overwinter outdoors, when grown in a pot it is easily moved indoors for a winter rest period. After frost danger is past in spring, move the pot outdoors, and the vine will rebloom.

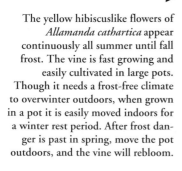

▶

The huge blossoms of angel's trumpets (*Brugmansia suaveolens*) bring a bold, tropical feeling to a garden. Tender perennials seen mostly in frost-free climates, angel's trumpets will also grow in containers farther north. Potted plants peg the corners of this formal Pennsylvania garden, above a border of annual coleus. The pots are hidden below ground and spend the winter in a frost-free greenhouse. Be aware that all parts of the plant are poisonous.

A mixture of tender and hardy perennials produces stunning foliage effects in a border that contrasts the slender leaves of ornamental grasses with the large, heart-shaped leaves of tender elephant's ears (*Colocasia esculenta*) and a bronze-leaf banana. Both the bulb that grows the elephant's ears and the rhizome that grows the banana plant can be dug up after frost and stored indoors over winter.

The grasslike foliage of New Zealand flax (*Phormium tenax*) beautifully complements ornamental grasses. Here, the variety Sundowner decorates a terra-cotta pot beside a formal pool overhung with hardy porcupine grass (*Miscanthus sinensis* 'Strictus'). The flax is susceptible to winterkill when subjected to severe freezes, so move it indoors after the first frosty days of fall.

This lush, tropical-looking garden exists on a Philadelphia rooftop. To create this look, grow the plants in containers and move them indoors during frosty months. The exotic foliage plants seen here include striped shell ginger (*Alpinia zerumbet* 'Variegata') and red-leaved mottled fire dragon (*Acalypha wilkesiana* 'Ceylon'). The flowering plants include hibiscus, impatiens, and lantana.

▼

Many southern cities suffer blistering hot, humid summers, but they enjoy a cool spring period, when many azaleas, dogwoods, spring bulbs, and perennial woodland wildflowers produce a crescendo of color. In this woodland garden, two kinds of wild blue phlox mingle with white foamflower (*Tiarella cordifolia*).

Persian buttercups (*Ranunculus asiaticus*) are spectacular cool-season bulbs for massing in beds in the Southwest, Southern California, and the Gulf States. The large blossoms of the Tecolote hybrids, shown here, are stunning. Ranunculus will not survive winters where the ground freezes, but northern gardeners can grow them in pots under glass.

▶

▶

The trumpet flowers of two similar flowering bulbs, both known as naked ladies, offer a welcome change from other late-season perennials. Hardy *Lycoris squamigera*, shown here, flowers in late summer, and tender *Amaryllis belladona* blooms in autumn. These plants produce leaves in spring that die back in summer. Later, the stalks arise from bare ground, causing another nickname, magic lily.

▲

This shady woodland planting mixes early-flowering perennials and biennials with interesting foliage patterns. Occupying center stage is a glorious spray of the cup-shaped green flowers of *Helleborus lividus*, a superb plant for cool but mild climates.

Though demanding of cool soil and cool spring temperatures to bloom, to survive it needs mild winters, such as those in the Pacific Northwest. The pink flowers of the variegated biennial money plant shine in the background.

Since many warm-season perennials are tender, some gardeners choose to grow them in containers. On a brick patio, pink-flowering crape myrtle (*Lagerstroemia indica*), blue mist shrub (*Caryopteris* × *incana*), and Burgundy Giant fountain grass make good companions. The light-colored brick acts as a heat trap, and it reflects light well to encourage flowering in pots.

Plants of gigantic proportions can be used as surprise elements in spacious gardens. The hardy hibiscus Southern Belle was hybridized from wild perennial swamp mallows, which grow along the Eastern Seaboard and throughout the Midwest. Producing dinnerplate size blooms in red, pink, and white, Southern Belle flowers the first year from seed, from midsummer to fall frost. This row of plants is sandwiched between clumps of tender elephant's ears in a New Jersey coastal garden.

Midwestern gardeners can look to the wild prairie for good midsummer-flowering perennials. In this meadow planting at the Chicago Botanical Garden, purple coneflower (*Echinacea purpurea*) and wild black-eyed Susans (*Rudbeckia hirta*), two prairie species, relish the sharp winters and warm, sunny summers; both plants thrive in a wide range of poor soils.

No hardy perennial seems to flourish in hot summers more than hybrid daylilies. The orange and yellow varieties seen here form a curving border that contrasts beautifully with varieties of blue spruce in the background. The cone-shaped evergreen planted in front of a springhouse is an Alberta spruce.

This gardener achieved the look of an English cottage garden with intensive plantings of foolproof hardy perennials. The plants seen here in their summer glory include purple loosestrife (*Lythrum salicaria*), orange Enchantment lilies, white beebalm (*Monarda didyma*), yellow perennial sunflower (*Helianthus × multiflorus*), and the tall, lime-green flower stems of lovage (*Levisticum officinale*).

Pink and blue tones create a cool, restful color harmony in a woodland garden in spring, with pink and white dogwoods extending floral color high into the sky. The blues are mostly self-seeding biennial forget-me-nots and perennial blue phlox, which has rapidly creeping roots. Azaleas and bleeding heart introduce bright splashes of pink.

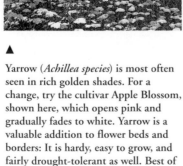

Yarrow (*Achillea species*) is most often seen in rich golden shades. For a change, try the cultivar Apple Blossom, shown here, which opens pink and gradually fades to white. Yarrow is a valuable addition to flower beds and borders: It is hardy, easy to grow, and fairly drought-tolerant as well. Best of all, it blooms for most of the summer.

Most of the perennials in this garden establish themselves quickly; this photo was taken only the second season after planting. Yellow yarrow, yellow evening primrose, English foxgloves, pink *Penstemon barbatus*, and silvery lamb's ears are all well established. The blue delphiniums and the pale yellow *Geum* 'Lady Stratheden' will need another season to fill out their appointed spaces because hot summers and harsh winters slowed their normal rate of growth.

▶

Cool weather during autumn in the Northeast can produce exceptional floral displays. Good fall bloomers for perennial gardens in this part of the country include pink-flowering *Aster novae-angliae* 'Alma Potschke' and purple-blossomed 'Treasurer', which, in this garden, billow and spill into a flagstone path between crimson panicles of annual *Amaranthus cruentus*. Creamy white flower spikes of perennial *Heuchera villosa* sparkle as an edging.

▼

A white picket fence helps to reflect light into this shady English-style cottage garden. The planting blends pale blue *Iris sibirica* with deep pink *Centranthus ruber* and the tall spikes of English foxgloves (*Digitalis purpurea*). Budding out in the foreground are plumes of false spiraea (*Astilbe* x *arendsii*).

◀

Bold clumps of red, pink, and white summer phlox (*Phlox paniculata*) and yellow swamp sunflower (*Helianthus* x *multiflorus*) maintain color throughout the summer in this New England garden.

▶

A backdrop of evergreen conifers, including spruce, junipers, and pines, helps to tie a midwestern perennial garden to its rugged, mountainous setting. Low, spreading hardy perennials are planted on the rock ledges of a manmade boulder-strewn mound. Coloring the garden in spring are pink and blue *Phlox subulata* and yellow broom.

▲

Here is a simple but effective pink and blue combination for a summer perennial garden. Both blue *Salvia officinalis* and rosy pink *Phlox maculata* 'Alpha' stand up well in the hot, sunny conditions of this midwestern garden.

▲

An ideal perennial for gardens in mountain areas is *Penstemon barbatus*, whose pink flowers are seen here in late spring. This rock garden in Colorado is planted with a combination of hardy perennials and dwarf conifers. Violet-blue *Salvia* x *superba* blooms with the penstemon, and blue junipers establish a decorative grove in the far distance.

Midwestern prairies are home to a large number of heat-tolerant perennial grasses and wildflowers, including summer-flowering gayfeather (*Liatris spicata*), which is planted at the center of this island bed. Surrounding it are reliable daylilies, shasta daisies, striped eulalia grass, and English lavender.

The raised porch of this clapboard home has little room for sophisticated plantings—just a strip of soil contained by a stone retaining wall. Usually, this kind of space is filled with uninspired annuals, such as scarlet sage, petunias, and red geraniums. Instead, this gardener allows *Heliopsis helianthodes* 'Scabra' to spill over the wall, covering the withered foliage of the Oriental poppies and spring bulbs that flowered earlier.

Plants brighten a shady corner, and a screen of trees and shrubs shelters this small city garden from a busy road. The shade-tolerant silvery foliage of bishop's weed (*Aegopodium podograria* 'Variegatum') edges the stepping-stone path, and a mixture of shade-tolerant *Aquilegia* 'McKana's Giant' blooms among garden ornaments that further help to light up the dark corner.

This herb garden shows an unusual planting combination suitable for the Midwest. Tender perennial scented-leaf geraniums (grown as annuals) contrast their attractive leaf shapes around the birdbath. Tall red-flowering *Amaranthus cruentus*, a tender annual, provides a strong decorative floral accent in the background.

In a small herb garden, fill every nook and cranny. In this garden, clumps of fragrant thyme are planted in cracks between the flagstones, so its spicy perfume is released when the leaves are bruised by feet. The bench is flanked by hardy pink beebalm and tender lemon verbena pruned to tree form. The verbena grows in a pot sunk into the soil and is taken indoors in winter.

A dramatic planting scheme for summer is suitable not only for the Midwest but also for the Northeast, in any sunny or lightly shaded location with moist soil, such as a pondside. This oval-shaped raised island bed at the edge of the woodland uses mostly hybrid varieties of *Astilbe*. White goatsbeard (*Aruncus dioicus*) towers in the background, while the massive blue-green leaves of *Hosta seiboldii* spill onto the lawn.

Ornamental grass gardens are perfect for the midwestern states because most perennial grasses tolerate heat, drought, and wind. This composition shows the autumn coloring of feather reed grass in the center, several varieties of maiden grass showing white and reddish flower plumes (*Miscanthus* species) in the background, and Japanese themeda in the foreground.

Here is an autumn perennial garden idea that makes a refreshing change from the ubiquitous cushion mums massed in island beds. A beautiful formal waterlily pool, it is the main display area at Gilbert Perennial Plant Nursery near St. Louis, Missouri. The terraced perennial borders in the background contain an assortment of autumn-flowering varieties, including white *Boltonia asteroides*, rosy-red *Aster novae-angliae* 'Alma Potschke', pink *Sedum spectabile*, and an assortment of ornamental grasses.

▼
Southern gardens need light shade, vine-covered walls, and lots of brick paving to maintain a cool environment for growing perennials through hot, humid summer months. Also, plants in pots are less prone to insect depredations. The centerpiece in this novel patio planting is a pedestal planter, overflowing with heat-tolerant *Echeveria elegans.*

▶
A collection of shade-loving, tender, rosette-forming bromeliads creates a spectacular composition of foliage colors. In the sunlight, a spiny blue century plant and columns of cacti contrast spectacularly with the bromeliad rosettes. Backlighting enhances the cactus display.

◀
Carry spring color high into the tree canopy with deep pink *Azalea indica,* a pale-pink flowering cherry, a rosy-pink flowering peach tree, and a yellow Lady Banks rose (*Rosa banksiae*), a tender perennial vine. The plants shown here mingle their blossoms along a woodland walk.

▲
A lovely blue-and-yellow spring motif for southern gardens is established with yellow tulips and wild blue phlox growing among the ruins of an old house. A perennial succulent, *Sedum lineare,* covers a pile of stones like a carpet of moss, soon to display yellow flowers. Live-oak trees are girdled with English ivy and draped with Spanish moss.

Old brick for paths and lawn edging is charming and is almost a trademark of southern gardens, especially in the historic section of Charleston, South Carolina. In a border of mixed annuals, perennials, and shrubs, a birdbath serves as a decorative accent, surrounded by yellow-flowering *Sedum lineare*, a drought-tolerant evergreen perennial that resembles cushions of moss.

Tender cat's claw vine (*Macfadyena unguis-cati*) is excellent for screening and cover; here, it drapes its large yellow trumpet-shaped blooms along the roofline of a garage. Cat's claw is spring blooming and is related to the hardy perennial trumpet creeper *Campsis radicans*, which can serve the same purpose in northern states (the yellow variety, Flava, is especially recommended).

Nowhere does Japanese wisteria (*Wisteria floribunda*) grow more vigorously than in the southern states, even scrambling up into the tops of lofty loblolly pines and massive live oaks. It can beautifully decorate a stone wall, like this one curtained with ivy. Note the fancy finial with its appropriate vinelike ornamentation, a clever detail introduced by landscape architect Beatrix Farrand.

This narrow Charleston garden concentrates color along its sides, where narrow beds grow a lavish assortment of flowering perennials, vines, and shrubs. A whippet dog sculpture looks out over an oval lawn outlined in old brick, and the sides of the property are hidden by camellias, azaleas, and jasmine vines. Pink tulips and old-fashioned George L. Taber azalea, white pansies, and white phlox establish a romantic pink-and-white motif between fence and lawn.

Though hardy only in frost-free areas such as southern Florida, fancy-leaved caladiums (*Caladium × hortulanum*) are popular bedding plants, since they relish the heat and humidity characteristic of southern summers. After frost browns the leaves, the bulbs are easily lifted and stored indoors over winter. Here, they are used to rim a waterlily pool.

Many flowering bulbs grown by northern gardeners as house plants can be enjoyed outdoors in the southern states. Here, in a Charleston city garden, a colony of amaryllis (*Hippeastrum* hybrids) blooms in spring after the azaleas have finished flowering. As long as the leaves are left to die down naturally, the plants will rebloom and multiply.

Although this footbridge, at Bellingrath Gardens near Mobile, Alabama, is on a scale too large for most home gardens, it serves to illustrate the versatility of cascading autumn-flowering chrysanthemums. Set into window box-planters below the bridge rails, the plants dip their blossoms into the water before cold weather ends the display.

Pots of white Easter lilies and tender perennial asparagus ferns (*Asparagus sprengeri*) beautifully decorate a southern courtyard garden like this one in New Orleans. The garden design takes inspiration from the Moorish gardens of the Alhambra Palace in Spain. Arching jets of water meet in a formal pool, shaped like a canal and fed by a narrow channel leading from a circular pool beside the lilies.

▶
The most heavily populated part of California—the Pacific Coast—enjoys a Mediterranean climate, allowing many tender perennials, such as pride of Madeira (*Echium fastuosum*), to overwinter. Here, in the courtyard garden at Carmel Mission, it contrasts its blue spires with the magenta flowers of Martha Washington geraniums (*Pelargonium domesticum*). Both are spring flowering.

▶
The famous desert wildflower displays occur in spring, and that's when West Coast gardeners like to concentrate a lot of color, mixing native annual wildflowers with introduced perennials. California poppies are California's state flower, and though they are annuals, their shimmering, satinlike petals make them perfect companions to iridescent perennial ice plants, such as *Drosanthemum roseum.*

▶
The California dream invariably involves a swimming pool in the landscape. Potted plants strategically placed at the corners and along the steps soften the hard architectural lines of this formal pool. Persian buttercups (*Ranunculus asiaticus*), pansies, and palms in containers grace the expanse of tile surrounding the pool.

▲
Make the most of a south-facing slope by building terraces. In this Los Angeles garden, landscape architect Robert Fletcher has established terraces connected by a horseshoe-shaped stairway that embraces a circular patio. Italianate sculptures and terra-cotta pots filled with succulents are strategically located along the steps and balustrades. Fall-blooming orange-flowered cape honeysuckle (*Tecomaria capensis*) decorates the foreground and controls erosion. White and pink forms of weeping lantana (*Lantana montevidensis*) cascade from the upper terrace. Eucalyptus and jacaranda trees, pruned of their lower branches to accentuate their trunks, add strong structural accents and light shade to break the force of the sun.

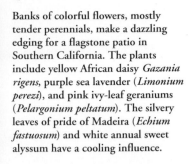

Banks of colorful flowers, mostly tender perennials, make a dazzling edging for a flagstone patio in Southern California. The plants include yellow African daisy *Gazania rigens*, purple sea lavender (*Limonium perezi*), and pink ivy-leaf geraniums (*Pelargonium peltatum*). The silvery leaves of pride of Madeira (*Echium fastuosum*) and white annual sweet alyssum have a cooling influence.

▲

A truly inspired plant combination for a warm climate: a colony of white calla lilies (*Zantedeschia aethiopica*) thrives under the shade of pink-flowering tamarisk and the cup-shaped, peach-colored blooms of *Abutilon hybridum*. In the background, held high into the sunlight by a trellised archway, the fragrant flower panicles of a wisteria create a misty dome of lavender-blue.

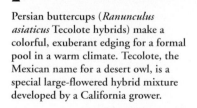

▲

Persian buttercups (*Ranunculus asiaticus* Tecolote hybrids) make a colorful, exuberant edging for a formal pool in a warm climate. Tecolote, the Mexican name for a desert owl, is a special large-flowered hybrid mixture developed by a California grower.

▲

The best California and southwestern perennial gardens seem to combine perennials with annuals. This spring display features perennial white shasta daisies (*Leucanthemum* × *superbum*) and red valerian (*Centranthus ruber*), enlivened with the sparkling white flowers of annual alyssum (*Lobularia maritima*), the shimmering golden cups of California poppies (*Eschscholzia californica*), and sunny yellow pot marigolds (*Calendula officinalis*).

Adobe walls roofed in Spanish tiles are characteristic of the architecture of parts of Southern California and the Southwest. An excellent plant to train on an adobe wall is the large-flowered, fragrant, shell-pink climbing rose Belle of Portugal. Too tender for freezing winter climates, this rose blooms in spring and tolerates heat and alkaline soil.

Southwestern gardeners can use the natural forms of drought-tolerant desert plants, including Sonoran palo verde trees (*Cercidium praecox*), to contrast with the clean architectural lines of a swimming pool. In this garden, its green trunks complement the lime-green flowers of *Euphorbia characias*. The silvery stems of a potted old man cactus and the blue-green pads of prickly pear cactus (*Opuntia*) also add interesting shapes and colors.

Xeriscaping is the technique of landscaping with drought-tolerant plants. Such landscaping is needed in this sunny border, where intense heat is reflected from a stone wall and a cement path, and the indigenous soil is sandy and highly alkaline, requiring a raised bed. Four plants that thrive here and flower in spring are orange *Aloe stricta*, red valerian, an old garden rose (Reine des Violettes), and yellow Spanish broom.

The tubular orange flowers of perennial red-hot poker plant (*Kniphofia uvaria*) beautifully complement the beige color of an adobe wall in a Spanish-style courtyard garden. Boulders of local sandstone create a raised island bed that holds improved soil. A clump of white shasta daisies (*Leucanthemum* x *superbum*) helps brighten the dark corner, shaded by a Golden Showers climbing rose.

Many parts of the Pacific Northwest have a climate and geology similar to those of Japan, so Japanese-style gardens fit into the landscape more successfully here than in other parts of North America. A large colony of Japanese iris (*Iris ensata*) creates a lovely scene in late spring, edging a pool fed by a cascade fringed with ferns and moss.

An alpine garden in a restful pink-and-blue motif fits beautifully into a hilly northwestern setting. This naturalistic alpine garden is tucked into a clearing among Douglas firs. Boulders, clumps of ferns, blue bugle weed (*Ajuga reptans*), and mountain pinks (*Phlox subulata*) create an unforgettable scene in early spring.

Carefully chosen plants transform a meadow garden into a tapestry of muted russet colors in autumn. The chestnut brown seedheads of *Polygonum* x *superbum* contrast with the straw-colored stems of spent Shirley poppies (*Papaver rhoeas*) and the silvery seedheads of goldenrod (*Solidago* species). The tall, dried flower stems of mullein (*Verbascum* species) connect the meadow to spires of evergreen conifers in the background.

Like a flow of lava, cushions of evergreen *Sedum acre*, purple creeping thyme (*Thymus praecox*), and pink thrift (*Armeria maritima*) cover a rocky slope in Washington State. In the background, beautiful weeping spruce resembles a waterfall. The spruce seems to melt into the sedum, while contrasting its smooth, flowing lines with the stiff spires of Douglas fir.

The combination of a cool northwestern climate and a sheltered location is perfect for the flowering of temperamental Himalayan hybrid primroses such as this *Primula* x *bullesiana*. An equally demanding species of bright yellow *Calceolaria integrifolia*, from Chile, makes a good companion; it blooms in the background in this garden created in an abandoned quarry.

For boggy sites use perennials that establish strong foliage accents. In this bog garden in Portland, Oregon, the large leaves of *Podophylum peltatum* spill into a small stream, edged with the spiky leaves of rushes, elegant fern fronds, and feathery horsetails (foreground). Subtle floral color comes from magenta-hued Japanese primula and yellow St.-John's-wort (*Hypericum calycinum*).

Nowhere do *Rhododendron* varieties grow better than in the Pacific Northwest. Create a bold color contrast by planting Spanish bluebells (*Endymion hispanicus*) between red hybrid Vulcan rhododendrons. Placing lighter colors (pastel peach, pale yellow, and white) in the background produces an illusion of greater distance because hot colors tend to project forward and cool colors recede.

The climate of the Pacific Northwest favors the growth of magnificent English *Delphinium elatum* hybrids. The pale silvery leaves of a variegated Norway maple accentuate the flower spikes and keep them from getting lost against a plain blue sky.

Chapter Four

Designing With Perennials

The decision to create beautiful garden designs with perennials is rather like graduating from colored crayons to oil paints. Like crayons, annuals and flowering bulbs are easy to work with, since they provide instant color. Many annuals flower non-stop, and their colors are intense. By purchasing ready-grown plants, it's possible to buy many annuals in bloom and to blend colors with ease.

Flowering bulbs rebloom each year, and the major classes, such as daffodils and tulips, are instantly gratifying. They burst into glorious bloom in early spring after a fall planting. Perennials tend to have a more sophisticated beauty than annuals or flowering bulbs, although the flowering period of many perennials is relatively short. Most will spread aggressively, so consideration must be given to the amount of space they will occupy after several years, and to orchestrating plantings so that as one plant passes its peak, another will come into bloom. Because it is so difficult to create an "ever-blooming" border with perennials, the best perennial borders tend to incorporate generous numbers of annuals and flowering bulbs as supporting players.

The first question in the design of any garden is whether to favor a formal or an informal design, or whether to incorporate the two styles.

Examples of highly formal designs are geometric-shaped beds, usually edged in boxwood, and plants placed shoulder to shoulder, in uniform heights, to create patterns. When defined by low hedges, these beds are known as *parterres.* Italian and French Renaissance gardens have some of the finest formal designs, and although these are not easy to emulate today because they require a large amount of space to look good, some small-space formal designs popular among the American Colonists can be shoe-horned into the smallest place.

The two most common formal planting designs during American Colonial times were known as the *quadrant* and *cartwheel.* The quadrant consists of a square space enclosed by a fence. Inside

the fence runs a border of mostly perennial plants (many of these were medicinal plants during Colonial days). The center of the space is divided into four or more squares dissected by a path. These inner squares contain mostly a mixture of annuals and perennials.

The cartwheel design features an outer circle and pie-shaped beds that meet in the middle. The central "hub" of the cartwheel is often a circular bed, but it can also be a structural accent, such as a sundial, a birdbath, or a wellhead. The bed dividers, or spokes, may be defined with bricks or stone, or even with low hedges of hardy perennial herbs. When curved in swirls, the bed dividers will criss-cross each other to make one of the most appealing of all formal garden designs: the *knot garden.*

Formal gardens tend to be enhanced by a formal water feature, especially a Florentine fountain or a rectangular waterlily pool.

Informal gardens eschew straight lines. Though the beds and borders may be sharply defined, creating circles, kidney shapes, squares, and rectangles, the plants are strategically placed to blur the edges. Informal gardens use lots of curving lines, and the visitor is led along by meandering paths. Plants are encouraged to spill into walkways and to dip their leaves into rocky streams. The edges of the property are deliberately disguised by a tapestry of greens, mostly from deciduous and evergreen shrubs and small trees.

The two most often used design elements in any perennial garden are beds and borders. A flower bed is usually an island of soil surrounded by grass, flagstone, brick, or some other surface material so that the plantings can be viewed unobstructed from several sides.

A flower border is usually a strip of soil backed by a hedge, a fence, or a wall and approached either along a path or across a section of lawn. Placed parallel, two perennial borders may be dissected by a path, so that the eye scans from one side to the other, taking in a feast of appealing color harmonies or color contrasts. The double perennial border—two borders separated by a path—is one of the most coveted floral designs in a flower garden.

The Perennial Border

Gertrude Jekyll's forte was the perennial border. Her borders consisted mostly of a long expanse of soil, backed by a stone wall or an evergreen hedge. She liked to see a succession of color through all the seasons, and she advocated planting perennial varieties in narrow clumps, or "drifts," so that as one group of flowers faded from bloom, a later-blooming variety could take its place. In her perennial borders, the soil generally sloped from the back to the front to better display the plants, and to aid drainage. Jekyll sandwiched medium-height plants between the tall background elements and used low, spreading plants as an edging.

The question of a background for borders is very important. A hedge tends to have a cooling influence and dissipates the force of winds much better than a wooden fence or a stone wall. High winds can easily jump over solid walls and wreak havoc, whereas a living hedge cushions the impact of high winds. Since the correct choice of hedge depends largely on location, it is best to consult local nursery people or to refer to a regional gardening book. Dark green evergreen hedges are wonderful backgrounds that highlight flowering plants, especially the silvery-foliaged and white-flowering kinds that Jekyll liked to use to soften harsh colors.

Stone walls have one big advantage over hedges: They provide strong support for an assortment of flowering vines. Walls tend to reflect heat and offer better frost protection than hedges. Though brick is favored in many of the best English perennial gardens, natural stone tends to look better in a North American landscape.

Perennial Beds

Island beds receive more sunlight, an even distribution of the water of natural rainfall, and good air circulation, generally allowing overall better growth for perennial plants than a border, where plants receive light from one direction.

Whatever the aesthetic choice—a bed or border—it is extremely important not only that the size be properly related to its surroundings, but also that the plants selected be in proportion to the space. The best perennial beds and borders feature several layers of plants: low, spreading kinds for edging, waist-high to chest-high plants for the main focus, and tall, towering plants at eye level and higher to form an interesting background. A fourth level—sky-high color, using climbers and vines—is the icing on the cake.

Foundation Plantings

The walls of a house are a favorite place to plant a perennial border. Because the house foundation may contain builder's rubble, it may be necessary to excavate to a depth of at least two feet so that plants can enjoy an adequate depth of good soil. Care should be taken that the eaves have gutters to catch rainwater, and that evergreens will not be damaged by snow falling off the roof. For under windows, choose low-growing shrubs that tolerate hard pruning so the view is not quickly obscured, and confine perennials to islands of soil between the woody plants. Foundation plantings that combine shrubs, perennials, and annuals are generally the most desirable.

Color Harmonies

A bed or border composed of many different colors is called a *rainbow planting*. Sometimes you can achieve a rainbow planting by using one perennial plant family (such as a mixture of tulips), but more often, you must combine an assortment of plants, incorporating the three primary colors—red, blue, and yellow—a triad color combination that is extremely popular in European parks. In a concentrated area, however, it's a good policy to think in terms of simpler color harmonies, such as pink and red, blue and violet, or orange and yellow. You can create monochromatic color harmonies (such as an all-white, all-blue, or all-red garden) by using not only flower colors but also foliage colors. Silvery foliage works well in an all-white garden; blue-green foliage, in a blue garden; and bronze foliage, in a red garden.

Garden Styles

The easiest style to recognize is surely the Japanese garden, which was influenced by ancient Chinese rock gardens. In the Japanese garden, an artistic arrangement is made of three essential elements: rocks, water, and plants. Usually, three-quarters of the plants in a Japanese garden are evergreen, to maintain year-round verdure and also to provide a background that accentuates the colors of flowers and foliage (especially the autumn foliage of selected deciduous trees, such as Japanese maples).

The antithesis of a Japanese garden is an English garden, best described as "organized chaos." For most American tastes, it is the English cottage garden, with its exuberance of floral color through all seasons, that is most desired. However, other ethnic garden styles exist, notably the Spanish style, which was influenced by Moroccan gardens and is especially suitable for parts of the South, the Southwest, and Southern California.

Container Plantings

In the world of politics, there is an old adage that says, "When all else fails, try money." In the world of gardening, when all else fails, try container gardening. When you garden in containers, it doesn't matter what kind of soil you have; just lay down a level wooden deck if the site is uneven, and group containers on it. Fill these with a good grade of commercial potting soil, mixed half and half with perlite or coarse builder's sand.

Virtually any kind of perennial can be grown in containers; your choices are limited only by the size of container. Ideally, containers for perennial plants should be made of clay or wood, since these are not overheated by a fierce sun, as metal and plastic often are. Whatever the container selected, it must have good drainage that allows excess water to escape and should be at least eight inches deep. If whiskey half-barrels are used, at least a dozen drainage holes should be drilled in the bottom.

A big advantage of containers is their portability. You can move hardy plants around to vary your planting scheme, and you can also move tender plants indoors for overwintering. The best container groupings combine plants of different heights and growth habits in different sizes of containers. Even tender flowering vines will grow rapidly in pots—and will flower continu-ously—provided they are given a strong trellis for support.

Hardy perennials must not be left exposed in pots during winter. If you don't have a cold frame or greenhouse in which to hold them, sink the pots in a raised pile of sawdust or shredded leaves so the rims are below the surface of the surrounding material.

A Fragrance Garden

A special bonus to seek from perennials is fragrance. Some peren-nial plants are rated highly for fragrance, such as English lavender (*Lavandula angustifolia*) and cottage pinks (*Dianthus plumarius*). Other plant groups not noted for fragrance may still include individual varieties that offer good fragrance. Among daylilies, for example, the old hybrid variety 'Hyperion' is pleasantly fragrant, and among hostas, 'Royal Standard' and 'Honey Bells' have exceptional fragrance. Conversely, some plant families noted for fragrance, such as carnations and roses, include varieties that have no fragrance at all (usually as a result of hybridizing).

A Cutting Garden

Where flowers are wanted for decorative floral arrangements, choose perennials with long, strong stems suitable for cutting, like gayfeather (*Liatris spicata*) and yarrow (*Achillea millefolium*). For everlasting cut-flower arrangements, seek out varieties with parts that dry easily. Many perennials have papery petals (such as the pearly everlasting, *Anaphalis triplinervis*), and the dried flowerhead itself is valuable for everlasting arrangements. Another large group of perennials has decorative seed pods (such as lotus and Siberian iris).

Water Gardens and Wetlands

Water gardens can be planted wherever there are natural ponds or streams, and these water features can also be made artificially, either to look natural, or to take the form of an artificial pool, channel, rill, or flume. The area bordering these water features can be raised suffici-ently above the watertable to be well drained, and to accommodate a vast number of perennials in beds of good garden soil. However, where the surrounding soil is permanently moist, boggy, or swampy, the garden designer must give thought to planting transitional perennials—plants that fill the gap between aquatic plants (such as waterlilies and lotus, which thrive permanently immersed in water) and bog plants (such as cattails and flag irises, which tolerate shallow water and swampy soil). In any wetlands habitat, short of draining the site and changing its natural state (an expensive proposition), it is far better to emulate nature and establish colonies of bog plants.

A swampy site can also be turned into a pond, though local per-mits may be needed if you are disturbing a stream or any area that can be designated a "wetland." The most beautiful pond plantings emulate the ancient Oriental concept of a *cup garden*, in which the pond surface is the bottom of the cup, and its surroundings form the sides. Thus, the surface of the pond can be planted with float-ing plants like waterlilies, and the pond margins can be planted with trees, shrubs, and herbaceous perennials of varying heights.

A Woodland Garden

Shade is the biggest problem in woodland gardens, along with acid soil. For a special discussion on shade, see Chapter 2. To tame wild woodland, first cut paths through it, and then make an inventory of any indigenous plants worth keeping (such as clumps of ferns, moss, and wildflowers). Where brambles and other suffocating undergrowth persist, clean them out and make clearings, pulling up noxious weeds by the roots so they will not regenerate. Woodland paths should be rustic and defined by a layer of mulch, such as pine needles or shredded pine bark—both a pleasant brown color and comfortable to walk on. The best woodland gardens have at least three levels of beauty: low groundcover plants to color the woodland floor, and small shrubs and small trees that act as an understory to the tall trees forming the highest level, the leaf canopy.

Meadow Plantings

Where a property is large, a quick and effective way to provide color is to create a wildflower meadow. There are two ways to establish a beautiful wildflower meadow, one expensive and the other less expensive. The best way—and the most expensive—is to plow the meadow and seed it in autumn with a mixture of wildflowers suitable for your area. Wildflower purists will want you to seed only indigenous wildflower varieties, but the only way to create a mix of indigenous species is to collect seed from the wild. Most wildflower mixtures purchased from seed companies contain a mixture of "introduced" wildflowers, mostly flowering plants from Europe and Asia that will "naturalize" in your area. Some popular components of these "introduced" wildflower mixtures include annuals for immediate effect. By plowing the entire meadow and seeding every inch of soil, you can expect to see a sea of wildflowers, the annuals coming on strong the first year, and the perennials dominating the second. After three years, this kind of planting may peter out as aggressive weeds and grasses crowd out the flowering plants, and so you must start again by plowing everything under and reseeding.

The less expensive method is simply to create islands of soil throughout the meadow and scatter your wildflower mixture onto the bare earth. You can seed some islands of soil with annuals, but the most beautiful and unusual effects will come from plugging the beds with perennial transplants.

A Garden in the Desert

The biggest problem of desert areas is lack of moisture. Where water rationing may be a problem, consider channeling natural rainfall into a reservoir by means of a water catchment. The roof of a house or a tennis court can serve double duty as a water catchment area. Highly alkaline soils and a subsurface hardpan called *caliche* are also problems, usually solved by creating raised beds surrounded by indigenous boulders and filled with good topsoil.

Plant selections for desert gardens should concentrate on cacti and succulents (plants with fleshy leaves that can survive long peri-ods without moisture). Though a major focus should be on forms with interesting, sculptural shapes, many also have exotic blooms.

A Rock Garden

Though desert gardens can take the form of a rock garden, the most famous rock gardens are those popularized by the British, and designed to simulate alpine rock screes—boulder fields with plants growing in pockets of soil. The best rock gardens feature a stream running through, with rock pools and cascades. A garden critic once described a rock garden as the greatest amount of work for the least amount of satisfaction. It is true that all the boulders and different levels make it difficult to cultivate and weed, and that alpine plants tend to be diminutive, but a well-designed rock garden, with dwarf conifers for foliage contrasts and some easy-care perennials (such as columbines, creeping phlox, and butterfly weed) in place of temperamental alpines, is one of the most uplifting sights in the horticultural world.

The Hillside Habitat

Beds and borders do not work in every situation. On a steeply sloping site, for example, soil would be washed away too quickly. For steep slopes, the best solution is the construction of retaining walls to make terraces. Plants should not only be placed in the level terrace section between the retaining wall and the slope, but they should also be planted in crevices between the bricks or stones. If the retaining wall is of dry construction (without cement), many drought-tolerant plants will readily root in the crevices. Where the brick or stone is cemented, pockets can be made to accommodate alpine plants, or trailing plants can be trained over the edge of the terrace to drape down the wall, softening the monotony of brick or stone. Less expensive wooden landscape ties can also be used to create retaining walls, but aesthetically they are not as attractive.

Allow a path to zigzag up the slope and to establish colonies of tenacious perennials on either side of the path by holding plants in place with netting until they are deeply rooted and knitted together. A dense mass of plants like this can control soil erosion. Where slopes are covered with trees, casting shade, the force of rain and wind is cushioned, and so pockets of good soil can be dug to accommodate wildflower plantings.

Coastal Gardens

These gardens can be found on exposed, rocky promontories, tucked among sand dunes, and surrounded by coastal wetlands. The nearness of the ocean is both a blessing and a hindrance. The biggest benefit is usually a cool climate that persists for most of the year, and the biggest challenge is the damage that can be inflicted by high wind and salt spray.

In many coastal gardens, sparse soil is a major problem. Where rocks prevail, a pickax may be needed to chip planting holes to hold good topsoil. At the other extreme, the soil may be too sandy and unable to hold moisture or nutrients, so mountains of compost, or well-decomposed animal manures, may be needed as a soil conditioner. Where the ground is too steep, terraces may have to be built, and if the site is too exposed, a windbreak of salt-tolerant shrubs must be established to cushion the force of the winds. While the windbreak plants are still young a temporary windbreak of hay bales or burlap strung between posts may be needed to shelter them.

Gardeners in warm, dry western climates looking for a naturalistic garden can simulate a chaparral planting of drought-tolerant perennials. The owners of this sunny Southern California slope have skillfully balanced perennials noted for their foliage effect with flowering kinds. The straight lines of a retaining wall and the rigid grid formed by patio tiles produce a strong division between softscape and hardscape. The dark green needlelike leaves of rosemary (*Rosmarinus officinalis*) and silvery lamb's ears (*Stachys byzantina*) are particularly effective in imitating the shrubby plants found in the nearby hills, while predominantly blue and yellow flowers provide colors common to the slopes of nearby canyons. Yellow yarrow (*Achillea filipendulina*), violet-blue hibiscus (*Alyogyne huegelii*), and a hybrid form of blue *Salvia clevelandii*—native to Southern California—are the principal flowering plants.

Designing a garden around an old tree gives a property a mature appearance impossible to create with nursery-grown plants. In this California garden, a native live oak (*Quercus agrifolia*) is ringed with an indigenous giant chain fern (*Woodwardia fimbriata*) and baby's tears (*Soleirolia soleirolii*) planted between random flagstones. The dark, spreading branches of the oak contrast dramatically with the lacy ferns and delicate baby's tears.

Woodland spaces are greatly enhanced by streams criss-crossed by stepping stones and bridges. The only plants indigenous to this site are the tall tulip poplar trees. Random plantings of Japanese azaleas, woodland ferns, hostas, and water iris replaced a tangle of brambles and look entirely natural.

At first, the owner was tempted to build a conspicuous arched wooden footbridge to span the stream but then decided it would be a distraction and would obliterate a pleasing vista. Instead, he spanned the stream with a simple wooden slab bridge placed below the level of the path, so that visitors step down instead of up. This bridge not only introduces a surprise element along the path, it allows the stream and its plantings to remain visible beyond.

Compact perennials can disguise a dry stone wall with glowing jewel-box colors. Spreading perennials with similar heights and flowering times give this carefully planned early-summer garden a free and informal appearance. The border begins with the blue shades of Dalmatian bellflower (*Campanula portenschlagiana*) and beach aster (*Erigeron glaucus*). It progresses through orange and yellow shades to the white of rock rose (*Helianthemum nummularium*), repeats yellow and orange, and ends in blue again, achieving a pleasing, symmetrical balance of color.

A stone retaining wall helps level a sloping site to make an informal, crescent-shaped perennial bed in a partly shaded area. A strategically placed English teak bench adds a functional structural accent, while an ivy-girdled tree provides a strong focal point. Cushionlike perennials, such as yellow lavender cotton, white baby's breath, and hostas in several shades of green, soothe the eye.

This garden space is made beautiful by a collection of plants representing one family. Rhododendrons and their smaller-flowered cousins, azaleas, are the most popular perennial shrubs for suburban gardens, especially in lightly shaded areas. The small brick patio with all-weather outdoor furniture is surrounded by flowering shrubs of different heights. The yellow potted azalea, an Exbury hybrid, is highly fragrant.

This barnyard has been turned into a delightful flower garden and outdoor dining area. Though the perennial beds are partly shaded by mature trees and a dark stone wall, the space is brightened with a paving of white landscape chips. The white-flowering slender deutzia (*Deutzia gracilis*) and lemon daylilies (*Hemerocallis citrinus*) both do well in light shade and add to the sense of brightness.

What do you do with an old, leaky swimming pool? Turn it into a sunken garden! The owner simply filled the cracked bottom with two feet of topsoil and softened the sides with dwarf evergreen shrubs. Then he planted a primrose path, using rough broken flagstone to further disguise the location. The bench provides a quiet, restful spot for reading and contemplation.

A clearing in the woods is a perfect spot for masses of blue forget-me-nots (*Myosotis scorpioides*) and wild blue phlox (*Phlox divaricata*), which reseed themselves. Yellow perennial alyssum (*Aurinia saxatile*) contrasts beautifully with the sea of blue. White-flowering dogwoods carry color high above eye level. An informal grass path the width of a lawn mower curves through the space to create a meadowlike feeling.

Though many formal gardens combine a formal layout with formal plantings, this small garden space combines a strong formal design with an informal plant arrangement. Note how the basic square design is repeated three times: first by the sundial, then by the flower bed, and again by the brick path. The pink-and-silver color scheme has a softening effect on the geometric design.

The combination of formal design and formal plantings was popularized in French Renaissance gardens. Located within a walled garden at historic Agecroft Hall in Richmond, Virginia, this grid design features pink and white tulips in regimented blocks of color. The rigidity of the design is slightly softened by a circular sundial and poodle-cut evergreen topiary accents.

Small formal garden spaces like this one look their best when the plants are chosen for a particular color theme or a simple color harmony. Here, mostly yellow-flowering perennials—yellow loosestrife (*Lysimachia punctata*), yellow sundrops (*Oenothera fruticosa*), and bush cinquefoil (*Potentilla fruticosa*)—create a yellow color emphasis.

The famous perennial garden at Wave Hill, New York, features a formal cartwheel design. Paths radiate from a central "hub" like the spokes of a wheel. Though many cartwheel designs have circular edges, the edges at Wave Hill are square. The raised central circle features *Phormium tenax* 'Sunrise', *Cepriosma kirkii variegata* (gold foliage), *Plectostachys serpifolia* (silver foliage), and cushion chrysanthemums.

▼

A low brick wall can elegantly define space in a formal garden, as in the sundial garden seen here. On the right the wall is straight, forming a terrace, while on the left, it follows the contours of a steep hill, creating a good transition from the formality of the garden to an open, naturalistic vista. The wall is high enough to shelter a bed of tulips from the winds that sweep up the valley.

◄

To design a formal garden, start by defining two strong, straight axes running perpendicular to each other, and design the garden around these axes. Shown here is the formal perennial garden at Wave Hill, New York, viewed along its cross-axis in early summer. For a view along the main axis in early autumn, see page 82. This garden space combines a formal design with an informality and exuberance in planting.

▼

A pergola is not only a wonderful formal element in a garden but allows a rich assortment of flowering vines, such as clematis, wisteria, and trumpet creeper, to be grown, along with hanging basket plants. Because the overhead struts and foliage cast heavy shade, a light-colored gravel is a wise choice for paving. Here, in the shady border edging a lawn, false spiraea (*Astilbe* × *arendsii*) alternates with heart-leaf bergenia (*Bergenia cordifolia*).

◄

The formal water garden at Wave Hill, New York, breaks with tradition by using only a small number of water-lilies, but a lot of ornamental grasses and grasslike plants, such as narrow-leaf cattails (*Typha latifolia*). All the plants growing from the water are in submerged tubs that control their proportions and maintain a clear expanse of reflective water.

Grouping tulips together by color in generous masses enhances a dramatic show in an informal mixed-bulb border at the edge of natural woodland. In the foreground, daffodils have finished blooming, but their leaves are left for at least six weeks so that the bulbs will be replenished. Tulips are popular for cutting, and as long as two leaves are left on a stem, the bulb can replenish itself to bloom again.

A decorative garden can double as a source of cut flowers if you cut judiciously. This lovely island bed on a California estate contains some favorite flowers for cutting. Mild winters allow tender Dutch iris (*Iris* x *hollandica*) and Persian buttercups (*Ranunculus asiaticus*) to overwinter. The decorative summerhouse with a pantile roof in the background matches the Spanish-style main house and guest cottages.

Thoughtful design is as important in a small garden as in a large one. This small bulb garden combines elements of naturalistic design and modernism. A meandering flagstone path leads to a formal bench, which contrasts effectively with a stone boulder. Heart-leaf bergenia (*Bergenia cordifolia*) harmonizes well with pink tulips, while white windflowers (*Anemone blanda*) spill into the path, softening its lines.

Bearded iris follow soon after the great tulip displays. They are sensational planted as bold ribbons of color in contrasting or harmonious colors. The flowers are especially effective when planted against an evergreen background, such as the dark green American arborvitae hedge seen here. When bearded iris flowers fade, the garden is left with the decorative fans of sword-shaped blue-green leaves.

Blue and yellow make a soothing color harmony for early summer. Parallel borders of English lavender lead the eye to an archway formed by a sheltering hemlock hedge. Masses of powder-blue catmint (*Nepeta* x *faassenii*) and violet-blue *Salvia* x *superba* create a sea of blue tones, while lady's mantle (*Alchemilla mollis*) and upright yews provide more subdued splashes of yellow.

This is surely everyone's idea of an English herbaceous border: a wide, straight planting area edged with a broken flagstone walk and backed by an evergreen hemlock hedge. Yet it is a private garden near Unionville, Pennsylvania. Individual varieties form generous clumps and are arranged by height to achieve a full, yet smooth flow of color and texture from front to back.

Where space is limited, parallel borders need not be planted far apart. In this narrow city plot, a brick path just six bricks wide slices through the garden, dividing the space into two equal parts; annuals, perennials, and evergreen shrubs spill into the path. A sundial and a sculpture of a maiden, staggered along the path, break up the mass of plants. Also to avoid monotony, the brick paving changes to flagstone midway down the path.

These double perennial borders create a sheltered sunken garden, and low stone retaining walls hold the soil in place. The curving walls are separated by a grass path leading to a tool shed that doubles as a focal point. Though perennials predominate (such as white baby's breath and yellow daylilies), the sloping borders are enriched with flowering annuals (particularly snapdragons and French marigolds) and dwarf evergreen boxwood. To break up the large expanse of siding on the main house, the owner has planted a bushy, white-flowering oak-leaf hydrangea. As the hydrangea's flowers fade, their petals turn pink and bronze, remaining decorative for most of summer and into autumn.

▲

A cartwheel design is an interesting way to structure a round garden. This circular island bed is the center of the cartwheel, and gravel paths radiate out between the pie-shaped beds. In the middle is a spring-flowering sweet-bay magnolia (*Magnolia virginiana*), encircled by false spiraea (*Astilbe* x *arendsii*). Golden marguerite daisies (*Anthemis tinctoria* 'J. C. Buxton'), white shasta daisies, and purple loosestrife add color to the foreground and background beds.

▲

One of the best examples of an informal perennial border is found at Glencoe Farm in Pennsylvania, the home of an expatriate Scot. The freeform border sweeps across a spacious lawn like a massive patchwork quilt. Watered by a built-in sprinkler system, the border is planted to reach peak bloom in early June, when the owner throws a lavish party to celebrate the floral display.

▶

Borders are good for underplanting arbors. Here, a romantic pink-and-blue color harmony is produced by parallel borders of English lavender, pink roses, and annual pink *Viscaria*. Wisteria vines twine around wooden columns supporting crossbeams. A large English teak Lutyens-style bench serves as a focal point, in scale with the flagstone paving.

These double perennial borders show the importance of low edging plants in softening straight lines. Separated by a wide flagstone walk, lots of low, spreading perennials have been deliberately placed at the front of each border to spill into the path. These include clumps of lime-green lady's mantle (*Alchemilla vulgaris*) and white dianthus. These borders feature a good balance of mound-shaped perennials (yellow and pink varieties of evening primrose, and white baby's breath) plus spirelike plants (such as red penstemon, pink veronica, and blue bellflower). The far border is partly backed by a hemlock hedge and a group of billowing apple trees, giving needed height to the otherwise flat terrain.

This small courtyard makes the most of a confined space by surrounding a central square bed with four borders separated by a narrow path. A sundial is the focal point, and the color theme is a subtle pink-and-silver motif, produced mostly by pink miniature roses, silvery lamb's ears (*Stachys byzantina*), and silvery pinks (*Dianthus* species).

What a wonderful way to say "welcome" to visitors! A simple concrete path is edged with autumn-flowering perennials, Autumn Joy sedum repeating itself several times to unify the design. Note that the straight path approaches the house at an oblique angle, enabling the occupants of the house to view more floral color than monotonous lawn.

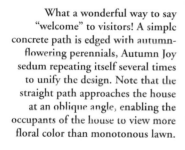

One of the most depressing sights on suburban and city lots is a boring driveway of black asphalt or gray concrete. Here, the owners of a two-car garage have solved the problem with a *landscaped* driveway, creating mixed perennial beds between the treadways. The perennials are alternated with dwarf evergreens and low boulders, so that when the perennials are out of bloom, the space between the treadways maintains horticultural interest. Vines trellised up adjacent walls help to decorate the dull expanses of brick.

▶

Herbaceous peonies make a lovely hedge. Here, old-fashioned pink and white peonies run the length of a perennial border backed by a stone retaining wall. Lavender-blue and purple bearded iris complement the fragrant peonies. Though the leathery peony leaves and sword-shaped iris leaves remain decorative all season, clumps of phlox, coreopsis, and other later-flowering perennials, edged by annual begonias, maintain color through the summer.

▼

Variegated shrubs make this small-space midsummer garden seem bigger than it really is because yellow and cream-colored foliage highlights in the rear border help the garden recede. A mixture of flowering annuals and perennials crowds two borders separated by a path of hexagonal tiles. Though shades of pink predominate, splashes of yellow and white echo the yellow and cream variegation in the shrubs to unify the design.

▼

The owner of this small-space perennial garden has a problem: a monotonous expanse of fence screening her property from a busy road. A border of tall perennials (including garden lilies and purple loosestrife) helps to some degree, but the finishing touch is a rope trellis woven with clematis, newly planted at six-foot intervals. With the benefit of a full growing season, the clematis will weave together and provide a beautiful flowering screen.

▶

Hostas and garden lilies are perfect companions in a shady bed. Here, the lilies are Mid-Century Hybrids, developed by famous Oregon hybridizer Jan de Graaff. The variegated hosta is Thomas Hogg, a variety that produces deep lavender-blue trumpet-shaped blooms.

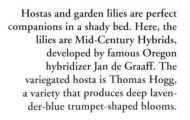

An English-style mixed-border features plants of different heights skillfully placed against an evergreen hemlock hedge. This garden within a garden is actually a secluded space planted for peak bloom in early summer. Shades of blue (dwarf anchusa, spiky veronica, and *Salvia* × *superba*) contrast well with shades of yellow (coreopsis, evening primrose, and *Digitalis* × *grandiflora*), planted in bold, irregular drifts.

Red and yellow together often create a garish contrast, but here the red cardinal flower (*Lobelia cardinalis*) and the yellow thread-leaf coreopsis (*Coreopsis verticillata*) are softened by silvery-gray lamb's ears (*Stachys byzantina*). Silver-foliaged plants are wonderful for toning down too strong a contrast, especially between primary colors.

The billowing flower clusters of a hybrid sedum, Autumn Joy, give substance and color to this late-summer perennial border. Silvery mounds of catmint overflow into a pink brick walk that echoes the color of the sedum. Misty blue spires of Russian sage and amber spires of feather reed grass add diversity to an understated autumnal planting scheme.

For a refreshing change from the gaudy pink and red evergreen kurume azaleas, consider planting fragrant mollis azaleas in pale yellow, orange, peach, and pink tones. Here, thread-leaf evergreen cypresses alternate between clumps of mollis azaleas along a house foundation.

For long-lasting color, mix annuals and perennials. This cheerful entrance planting is a ribbon of color that peaks in late summer. Perennial pink *Sedum spectabile* is repeated on both sides of the entrance, while perennial *Artemisia* 'Silver King' weaves between clumps of annual gloriosa daisies and annual French marigolds. Other old-fashioned flowers, such as nasturtiums and hostas, complement the Victorian charm of the house.

Without the edging of bright pink mountain phlox and the white highlights, the cushions of mostly red evergreen azaleas would be a rather mundane foundation planting. White perennial candytuft, white phlox, and a single clump of white azaleas all help to echo the white siding, while the red accents complement the reddish brown shutters and the burnt orange roof.

For a really different look, try an unusual color scheme, like this mono-chromatic color harmony of pink, magenta, and purple. This warm-climate garden uses tender perennials to striking effect. The edging is *Crassula multicava*, an easy-care succulent. Pots of daisylike cinerarias are sunk into a raised bed behind them, and purple and white violas define a transitional zone between the crassulas and the cinerarias.

It's hard to beat tulips for early spring color, since tulips have the richest hues and the most extensive color range among spring-flowering bulbs. Here, solid-colored Triumph tulips are mixed with bicolors for maximum interest. Blue grape hyacinths, used as an underplanting, help intensify the tulip colors. Note the tulip arrangement inside the window.

Foundation plantings don't have to be straight. This semicircular bed at a seaside cottage has blue lace-cap hydrangeas against the house and a crescent of yellow daylilies. Just about to bloom in the center of this grouping are spires of orange tiger lilies. All these perennials are summer flowering and salt tolerant.

Not only are the broad leaves of hostas decorative in themselves, but in summer, these shade-tolerant plants offer the bonus of beautiful tubular flowers on long stems. Here, the owner contrasts a matte-blue variety with a lustrous green to establish a cooling effect along a brick walk.

Surrounding a freeform lawn with mixed flower borders of annuals, perennials, and small shrubs is not a particularly novel idea, but what is unusual about this design is the series of small water gardens that have been incorporated into the border along the left-hand side, each with a flagstone edging that helps to make a view of the garden more visually exciting.

A garden of all-white flowers is refreshing on a hot day, and it sparkles in summer twilight. One of the world's most beautiful and famous perennial gardens is this white garden created by Vita Sackville-West at Sissinghurst Castle in England. A canopy of white climbing roses, white delphiniums, white pansies, and silvery lamb's ears are strong components of this view along the main axis. Variegated obedient plant (*Physostegia virginiana*) and blue-green blades of European dune grass shimmer white in the sunlight. White gardens are sometimes called *moon gardens* because white flowers reflect the light of the moon, creating a romantic quality. Sackville-West herself hoped that one night she might see a ghostly white barn owl fly across her white garden.

Here is a well-balanced monochromatic yellow composition where the yellow theme is echoed in an adjacent flower bed. In the foreground are yellow Asiatic hybrid *Lilium* 'Nutmegger' and golden marguerites (*Anthemis tinctoria*), which repeat in the facing bed. Note how the yellow in the facing bed changes to blue, with lime green *Alchemilla vulgaris* used as an edging to effect the transition.

In the artistic world, *monochromatic* means the use of only one color. In the horticultural world, the meaning of *monochromatic* is stretched to include *tones* of one color. And of course, there is almost always the presence of green, the predominant color of foliage. In this pink garden, the pink tulips and azaleas are accentuated by the presence of white pansies and white stocks.

In plans for a monochromatic garden, the use of contrasting flower shapes and plant habits prevents the monotony that can occur in single-color plantings. This gardener introduced visual excitement with the globe-shaped, deep pink flowers of giant allium. Held high on long, slender stems, and seemingly floating in midair, they contrast well with the paler pink spires of lythrum behind, and the low, frosted rose-pink flower clusters of China Doll roses.

Analogous color schemes use closely related colors, such as red and purple, blue and violet, and yellow and orange. The artist Claude Monet was particularly skillful in creating analogous color harmonies in his garden at Giverny, France. In this midsummer planting, yellow gazanias, Mid-Century Hybrid lilies, and yellow loosestrife create a dramatic orange-and-yellow composition.

Pink and blue create a classic color harmony. In this intensively planted early-summer border, the pink is produced mostly by miniature roses, such as The Fairy, and the blue comes from *Geranium pratense*, *Nepeta* × *faassenii* and *Lavandula angustifolia*. White and silver are interspersed among the blues and pinks to help soften the display, giving it a misty, romantic feeling.

One of the most unusual color-theme gardens is a "silver garden," using mostly silvery foliage effects. In this striking composition, the centerpiece is a clump of tender silver leaf (*Plectranthus argentea*), flanked by two varieties of wormwood (*Artemisia species*) and silvery cardoon (*Cynara cardunculus*). In the background are purple-flowering Mexican sage (*Salvia leucantha*) and white feverfew (*Chrysanthemum parthenium*). The tiny purple flowers of wild sage (*Salvia scabra*) and French lavender (*Lavandula dentata*) echo the purple stems of the silver leaf and the purple flowers of the cardoon and the Mexican sage.

Some gardeners like to plant around their favorite color, as did the late Ganna Walska, who created a magnificent pink tropical garden at her home, Lotusland, in Santa Barbara, California. She surrounded her estate with a pink wall, painted the house exterior pink, and planted a pink garden composed of tender succulents. This portion of her garden features light pink *Crassula multicava* (foreground) and a deeper pink *Cotyledon orbiculata* (background), both drought-tolerant spring-flowering plants. Boulders and gravel simulate an arid environment, and a pair of figurines adds a whimsical accent.

Here is an interesting late-summer monochromatic combination for a drought-tolerant garden. The late Thomas Church, a California landscape architect, devised this duet of sedums. Note how the deep pink coloring of *Sedum* 'Autumn Joy' and the rich carmine of *Sedum* 'Ruby Glow' complement the red coloring of the brick path. Spanish dagger (*Yucca filamentosa*) creates a good foliage contrast in the rear.

A stunning analagous color harmony for early summer blends the deep violet-blue flowers of *Veronica incana* 'Goodness Grows' with the feathery pink plumes of *Astilbe* x *arendsii*. In addition to good color tones, these varieties have strong leaf contrasts: a bright green, fernlike effect in the astilbe and a blue-green, spear-shaped leaf in the veronica.

Subtle introductions of other colors can enhance a color scheme. In this silver garden at Wave Hill, New York, the pale lavender-blue flowers of *Aster novae-angliae* harmonize softly with gradations of silvery foliage. The silver-white lamb's ears in the foreground are the common *Stachys byzantina*, while the larger-leafed variety behind is a special silvery gray selection known as Wave Hill. A feathery aromatic hybrid wormwood (*Artemisia* 'Powis Castle') is a perfect foil for the aster flowers, and a clump of low bronze foliage, introduced as an edging, cleverly strengthens the silvery effect.

Blue and yellow together create one of the most easily planted bicolor combinations for summer, since so many yellow and blue flowers bloom at that time. At center stage is *Salvia* x *superba* 'Lubeca', accentuated by pale pink *Boltonia* 'Pink Beauty'. Spires of yellow loosestrife (*Lysimachia punctata*) and star bursts of yellow *Rudbeckia* 'Irish Eyes' provide just the right shade of buttercup yellow.

All-blue gardens are one of the most difficult monochromatic color themes to achieve because a true sky-blue is one of the least common colors in the plant kingdom. In this island bed, a blue motif is achieved by violet-blue *Salvia* x *superba* (foreground), the lilac-blue biennial *Salvia sclarea* (rear), deep blue *Campanula latifolia* (right), and the powder-blue biennial *Jasione laevis* (extreme left).

This all-red color theme not only makes a dramatic display but is achieved by plants also suitable for cutting. They include *Achillea millefolium* 'Fire King' (foreground), *Penstemon* hybrid 'Garnet' (right), *Monarda didyma* 'Cambridge Scarlet' (center), and *Lilium* Asiatic hybrid 'Cinnamon' (rear).

Orange and violet make a striking color contrast. Though tender, and suitable only for mild-winter areas such as Southern California, the orange flower clusters of *Aloe saponaria* and purple-flowered sea lavender (*Limonium perezii*) are perfect partners. They are both tolerant of salt spray and drought, blooming in early spring.

Though purple loosestrife (*Lythrum salicaria*) and its hybrids are banned in some northern states, where the plants become invasive in boggy soil, it is a striking perennial for midsummer, especially when planted with red beebalm (*Monarda didyma* 'Cambridge Scarlet'). Both flowers are highly attractive to hummingbirds.

In traditional Japanese gardens, water, rocks, and green plants are skillfully combined to create artistic effects. Here, along a small rocky stream, evergreen lilyturf (*Liriope spicata*) forms grasslike tussocks, contrasting with clumps of feathery fern fronds and the sharply indented leaves of astilbe. Spires of blue bugle weed (*Ajuga reptans*) have a subtle, mistlike quality, and though the red kurume Japanese azalea strikes a discordant note, the floral colors are sufficiently understated to balance the dominant green of the composition.

In order to create a strong Japanese theme garden, it's not necessary to have a lot of authentic Japanese plants. Here, at the Chicago Botanical Garden, an emphasis has been placed on structural elements, with a stepping-stone path leading across a moss lawn toward a teahouse. The bold blue-green leaves of perennial hosta contrast with the delicate light green perennial fern fronds and the needlelike leaves of artistically pruned pine trees.

In woodland spaces, where a strongly acid soil and dense shade make it difficult to grow grass, moss is often the best alternative. Here, cushions of perennial mosses, used as an evergreen groundcover, contrast naturally with the hard, strong lines of boulders. The rustic gazebo—though Japanese in design—is not a dominant Oriental feature, and it does not seem out of place in this Pennsylvania landscape.

▼
Only a small number of flowering perennials are favored in traditional Japanese gardens, since the design emphasis is usually on foliage contrasts for quiet contemplation. Anything loud, garish, or bizarre, particularly color mixtures, is avoided. Summer-flowering Japanese water irises (*Iris ensata*), like these, are greatly admired because their elegant sword-shaped leaves contrast well with other pondside plants such as ferns and mosses.

▲
Traditional Japanese gardens tend to be too manicured for most Western tastes, with their sharply defined flagstone paths, carefully weeded moss groundcovers, severely clipped "cushions" of azaleas and camellias, and meticulously raked expanses of gravel symbolizing inland seas. This more naturalistic interpretation of a Japanese-style garden has a more carefree appearance, with evergreen ivy and perennial tussock grasses spilling over the edges of a boulder-rimmed reflecting pool. Only one design accent—a stone lantern—suggests a definitive Oriental flavor. Take away the stone lantern, and the design still stands as a beautiful woodland garden, with a clump of tender perennial calla lilies presenting an appealing floral accent among predominantly foliage contrasts.

▶
Authentic Japanese-style gardens are sometimes difficult to emulate because of cost or because the plants favored by garden designers in that country are unsuitable for a particular climate. Appropriate substitutions are sometimes necessary to create a similar impression. Here, perennial bearded iris substitutes for Japanese water iris to simulate a Japanese water garden.

▶

Limitations of space do not prevent Japanese or Chinese garden masters from creating appealing vignettes of water, stone, and foliage. Here, an artistic arrangement of rocks creates a small water catchment to support an arrangement of beautiful foliage plants, including perennial male fern (*Dryopteris filix-mas*), dwarf white pine, dwarf blue juniper, and dark green Japanese holly.

▼

It's a fact that structures in a garden can more quickly establish a theme than plants alone. This is particularly true of Oriental gardens, where the placement of a single ornament says "Japanese" or "Chinese." In this frost-free garden, where a Japanese cycad palm, heart-leaf Japanese butterburr, and *Asparagus sprengeri* fern help establish a subtle tapestry of greenery, the golden shrine and the stepping-stone path add a definitive Oriental stamp to the design.

▲

Japanese garden designers consistently contrast hardscape material (stone, gravel, and wood) with softscape (plants), allowing the two to merge in a bold contrast of textures. Here, the fresh green spring growth of perennial hosta encroaches on a path of round, flat stepping stones set into a gravel base. An underplanting of dark green Japanese spurge (*Pachysandra terminalis*) enhances the hosta foliage.

Perhaps nothing exemplifies an English garden more than a mixed double perennial border. Here, the richly planted borders are approached through a tunnel of branches so that the flowers appear as an oasis of light. Though the borders feature strong splashes of red, deep pink, and blue, the plant palette is lightened by islands of white (from *Salvia sclarea*) and the translucent pale pink petals of showy primrose (*Oenothera speciosa*).

The British are fond of playhouses, which serve as decorative accents for gardens of mixed perennials and annuals in "cottage-garden" style. This Tudor-style thatched cottage is at Old Westbury Gardens, Long Island, in a garden space defined by a white picket fence. A colorful border of white perennial shasta daisies and pink astilbe has an edging of pink annual begonias and yellow French marigolds.

The British climate allows gardeners to use temperamental alpine gems, such as gentians, in their rock gardens, while most Americans are limited to rock garden perennials that endure hot, dry summers. This rock garden at Longwood Gardens, Pennsylvania, features low-growing white rock cress, mountain pinks, yellow perennial alyssum, blue bugle weed, and dwarf yellow irises massed in drifts to create the illusion of an alpine meadow.

The long-lasting lime-green flowers of lady's mantle (*Alchemilla vulgaris*) are a perfect edging for English perennial gardens. Here, they echo the yellow-tinted evergreen leaves of a dwarf golden cypress and help to cover up the lower parts of tall blue delphiniums and paler violet-blue *Campanula lactiflora*. An orange-flowered Enchantment Asiatic hybrid lily and a touch of silver from lamb's ears complement the blue tones.

Here, in an English-style perennial garden on a gentle slope, beautiful color harmonies are made by large plantings like daubs of paint splashed across the landscape. The analogous colors in this planting are red valerian (*Centranthus ruber*) and lavender-blue *Salvia pratensis*.

The approach of autumn need not mean the end of perennial color. In areas too tender for pampas plume to survive, *Miscanathus sinensis* 'Silver Feather', with its silky white flower plumes, is a good substitute. Here, at Wave Hill, New York, late color is also supplied by perennial blue oat grass, pink Fairy roses, fountain grass, sparkling white blossoms of *Gaura lindheimeri*, and a late-blooming yellow daylily.

Woodland gardens are generally most colorful in early spring because many perennial plants, such as these English primroses (*Primula vulgaris*) and American foamflowers (*Tiarella cordifolia*), sprout from winter dormancy, flower, and set seed before the tree leaves fully unfurl to cast the garden into deep shade.

In North America, nothing beats a sheltered coastal location for the spectacular flowering performance of perennials favored by the British. Here, a riot of spring color in a Carmel, California, garden is produced by purple English foxgloves, two-tone bearded irises, and red penstemon. Scarlet sweet peas and golden California poppies add a touch of annual color to this terraced mixed border.

Rose-covered arbors are almost a trademark of English cottage gardens. Here, an informal rustic arbor garlanded with climbing roses frames a raised bed planted with annual pansies and snapdragons. Perennial creeping Jenny (*Lysimachia nummularia*) cascades over the retaining wall like a curtain. A matching rose arbor at the far end of this garden not only provides an attractive focal point but marks a change in color scheme, from bright yellows and reds to cool whites and blues.

British gardeners like to use certain large herbaceous plants as sculptural accents. In this English-style perennial garden, a single specimen of biennial Scotch thistle (*Onopordum acanthium*) adds a strong structural quality, its stiff blue-green stems towering dramatically above a gently curving grass path and cushions of colorful medium-height perennials.

The owners of this English-style perennial garden have chosen a distinctive gazebo of their own design to serve as a focal point for two parallel beds separated by a brick path. It may be best to avoid gazebos produced from a kit, as many mail order designs tend to be over-familiar and can "cheapen" even the most elegant flower borders.

Containers made of tufa rock (a porous rock ideal for growing alpine plants) are frequently used as accents in small garden spaces in Britain. Indeed, the making of "trough" gardens is a favorite British pastime. In this intensively planted island bed, the owner has used tufa rock as a pedestal planter for a collection of alpine plants, and several trough planters (both round and rectangular in shape) are strategically placed around the edges of the bed.

The key to making a cottage garden is an abundance of plants. Incredibly, this cottage garden at Cedaridge Farm, Pennsylvania, had been a mere patch of lawn three months earlier. Planted in May with mail-order shipments of quick-blooming perennials, and with annuals that were seeded directly in position, the space is alive with brilliant color in midsummer. Perennial white shasta daisies, orange-and-red gaillardia, yellow black-eyed Susans, pink lupines, and biennial white foxgloves occupy the fenced-in area. Fragrant roses underplanted with English lavender flower in the background. Annual pink petunias cascade from an antique urn, and cherry red nasturtiums weave through the beds and spill into the winding grass path.

Tender plants can create the look of an English cottage garden in a warm climate. The owners of this California estate maintain the flower beds with year-round color, using a plant palette that includes perennials too tender for colder areas. For this "cottage garden" in spring, flowers have been chosen not only to provide colorful garden display, but also for cutting. They include blue Dutch irises, pink and yellow Persian buttercups, blue and white delphiniums, and white marguerite daisies. A bed of white snapdragons gleams in the background.

In English cottage gardens, old-fashioned blue delphiniums and antique varieties of pink garden roses seem to go together like strawberries and cream. These are especially good for decorating the walls of cottages and old tool sheds, as seen here. Modern gardeners have the advantage of new Heritage roses, possessing a strong fragrance and extraordinary vigor, and developed by renowned English rosarian David Austin.

This formal sunken garden was inspired by designs created by the late great British architect Sir Edwin Lutyens, who worked in collaboration with Gertrude Jekyll to create many beautiful garden spaces. The "bowed" steps are a Lutyens trademark. Curved flower beds surround a fountain, creating a classic "cartwheel" design. Originally intended as a rose garden, this garden space was converted to an herb garden, and all the perennial plants featured here have culinary or medicinal value.

Where the soil is unsuitable for plants, raised beds make a garden possible. This small cottage garden is planted on a shelf of hard shale. Where the shale is close to the surface, raised beds made from economical landscape ties increase soil depth. Silvery lamb's ears and other silver-leaved, cascading perennials not only camouflage the sides but complement the shell pink Simplicity roses planted along the white picket fence.

Potted plants can be used to decorate a path or stairs. Steps leading down to a swimming pool from the main house at the former Richard Nixon estate, Casa Pacifica in San Clemente, California, are decorated with a wealth of spring-flowering perennial bulbs and multi-colored pansies in containers. The terra-cotta tub in the foreground, filled with Persian buttercups (*Ranunculus asiaticus*), and all the other terra-cotta pots match the brickwork.

Hyacinths are highly fragrant spring-flowering bulbs that are best planted close to the house so that their gardenialike fragrance can be fully appreciated. To decorate a redwood deck, a mass of the hybrid Pink Pearl has been planted in a low, dish-shaped container. The combination of the marbled blue coloring of the container and the bright pink hyacinth flowers creates a sophisticated contrast.

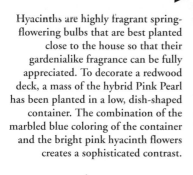

Normally associated with woodland gardens and mixed perennial borders, where they can reseed themselves freely, biennial English foxgloves make sensational container plants to decorate decks and patios. Their rocketlike flower clusters carry color high above the limits of most other flowering plants.

The challenge of creating an exciting container garden can be met by using size, color, and form as design elements. Here, a downtown Philadelphia roof-top is turned into a tropical oasis by the contrast of silvery succulents and spiny cactus with the lush paddle-shaped green leaves of a dwarf banana and the marbled pink foliage of *Acalypha wilkesiana* 'Macafeana'. The owner deliberately used clay pots to emphasize the decorative qualities of his exotic plant collection. The floral color is subdued, confined to an apple-blossom geranium and a hybrid fuchsia.

The crevice of a large boulder makes a perfect home for a colony of drought-tolerant hen-and-chickens (*Echeveria* species), a hardy perennial succulent that is closely related to sedums, two varieties of which surround the base of the boulder: yellow-flowered *Sedum acre* and white *Sedum brevifolia*.

Containers offer an opportunity to introduce a touch of whimsy to a garden. Here, a terra-cotta cockerel sports a handsome set of wings from a healthy colony of hen-and-chickens (*Sedum sempervirens*). Each of the "chickens," or offsets, can be removed to create a new colony.

A combination of hanging baskets and window-box planters can create a vertical garden. The walls of a lake shore summer home support this collection of summer-flowering annuals and tender perennials that spend the winter in a lean-to green-house around the back. The plants here include hybrid fuchsias, ivy-leaf geraniums, and tuberous begonias.

Many culinary herbs have drab flowers but interesting leaf shapes and textures. Here, the lustrous spear-shaped leaves of hardy French sorrel contrast with the sharply indented, velvety leaves of two kinds of tender scented-leaf geranium, one a plain green and the other variegated with silver. *Fraises de bois* (strawberries), spear-shaped sesame leaves, the needlelike foliage of a weeping rosemary, and a bushy spearmint help to produce a soothing tapestry of foliage effects.

Tuberous begonias are fast-growing, shade-tolerant plants that maintain a spectacular display all summer. Thus, they are ideal for decorating covered porches and patios. The beautiful hybrid specimen seen here growing in a whiskey half-barrel is watered daily so that the soil stays cool and moist. Though tender, the doughnut-size tubers can be lifted after frost kills the top growth and can be stored indoors over winter.

Many kinds of azaleas are suitable for growing in containers. For the northern states, the evergreen Japanese varieties, such as the kurume hybrids, are especially beautiful. In warmer climates, such as Southern California and the Gulf States, heat-tolerant Indica azaleas are the preferred choice. This handsome bicolor is an Indica type, Southern Charm.

These terrestrial fairy orchids (*Pleione bulbicodium*) are reasonably hardy perennials that grow from bulbs, but they tend to get lost when planted out in the garden. Here, on a San Francisco terrace, they have been used in the shade of a tender cycad palm (*Cycas revoluta*) in a tall urn that elevates them closer to eye level.

Vining ivy-leaf geraniums have the advantage of flowering continuously all season. Though they are tender perennials, they are easily trimmed back and moved indoors for protection from freezing weather. They are especially good cascading plants for decorative urns.

Florists' cyclamen are tender, temperamental plants, but many small-flowered species are hardy. They tolerate light shade, and though they can be planted out in the garden, especially along woodland paths and in rock gardens, they tend to get lost in competition with other plants. Planted in containers and set on a pedestal beside a patio, they are eye-catching.

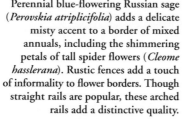

Perennial blue-flowering Russian sage (*Perovskia atriplicifolia*) adds a delicate misty accent to a border of mixed annuals, including the shimmering petals of tall spider flowers (*Cleome hasslerana*). Rustic fences add a touch of informality to flower borders. Though straight rails are popular, these arched rails add a distinctive quality.

The most enduring and most colorful flower borders combine perennials with annuals, especially everblooming annuals such as the impatiens used as an edging in this design. The perennials include yellow black-eyed Susans (*Rudbeckia fulgida*), silvery wormwood (*Artemisia ludoviciana*), and a young climbing rose, Don Juan, that spreads its canes along the split-rail fence by season's end.

For autumn color, it's hard to beat tuberous dahlias and New England asters. In the mixed flower garden at Wave Hill, New York, the "everblooming" Bishop of Llandaff dahlia displays scarlet flowers against bronze foliage, while a purple New England aster, The Treasurer, makes a strong accent at the end of the flagstone path. White-flowering *Nicotiana sylvestris*, a tall tender annual, displays pendant white flowers.

Aptly named meadowfoam, for the fluffy texture of its bright pink flowers, *Filipendulina rubra* is a spring-blooming hardy perennial. Rising through an underplanting of blue biennial forget-me-nots, and accentuated by the bright orange and yellow petals of annual California poppies (*Eschscholzia californica*), the meadowfoam stands out like cotton candy at a carnival.

◄

Taking advantage of a steep drop in elevation, the owners of this small courtyard garden overlooking Monterey Bay in California built two raised planting beds of brick for growing annuals and perennials. The beds are separated by steps leading to a bench. Perennial chamomile (*Chamaemelum nobile*), a tough, mosslike groundcover planted between the flagstones, releases its spicy, apple-scented perfume when walked upon.

▲

The number of flowering perennials suitable for shade diminishes as summer progresses. At Prescott Park, along the riverfront at Portsmouth, New Hampshire, everblooming annual impatiens occupy shady areas, while islands of sunlight glow with sun-loving perennials, such as black-eyed Susans (*Rudbeckia fulgida*) and perennial sunflower (*Helianthus* x *multiflorus*), seen here.

►

Hardy annual California poppies, with their shimmering orange petals, enliven perennial beds in early summer, even in the East. This garden also features red *Centranthus ruber*, silvery wormwood (*Artemisia ludoviciana*), and mauve Siberian wallflower (*Erysimum* 'Bowles Variety').

◄

A dramatic plant can make an ordinary garden special. This clump of orange tiger lilies (*Lilium lancifolium*) turns a rather mundane small-space planting of annual geraniums and zinnias into a prize-winning summertime flower garden in a coastal community in Massachusetts.

A rim of hardy perennials and summer-flowering bulbs encloses a small-space vegetable garden, where sugar snap peas are trained up a trellis. The foreground is a rainbow planting of tuberous dahlias, perennial feverfew, and annual candytuft. The right side has an all-white theme featuring white perennial *Astilbe* x *arendsii*, white perennial feverfew, and white biennial foxgloves.

Japanese bleeding heart (*Dicentra spectabilis*) is a wonderful early-spring-flowering perennial for adding interest to bulb plantings because its graceful indented foliage and elegant arching flower stems offer a pleasant contrast to the stiff stems and erect spear-shaped leaves of tulips.

The electric colors of some flowering bulbs sometimes need toning down with darker colors and foliage accents. Here, multicolored Persian buttercups (*Ranunculus asiaticus*), a tender flowering bulb, share a bed with perennial Siberian wallflower, *Erysimum* 'Bowles Mauve'. The bronze foliage of perennial New Zealand flax (*Phormium tenax*) adds a dramatic foliage accent to the composition.

Bicolored flowers are easy to work into color schemes if you repeat one of the colors with other flowers. Yellow daisylike flowers of hardy perennial dogbane (*Doronicum caucasicum*) complement the bicolored yellow-and-scarlet flowers of Kees Nelis tulip in a foundation planting that includes a weeping pear tree and a firethorn for background interest.

Perennial Mexican cardinal flower (*Lobelia fulgens*), which has blazing red flowers, is less hardy than the American cardinal flower (*Lobelia cardinalis*), but it has distinctive bronze foliage that is a useful design element. Here, the foliage complements the hot rainbow colors of summer-flowering tuberous dahlias. Annual painted daisies (*Chrysthanthemum carinatum*) decorate the foreground.

Lilies are classic summer flowers, but some bloom late enough for fall gardens. The beautiful white trumpet-shaped flowers of this late-season lily (*Lilium formosanum*) tower above perennial New England asters (*Aster novae-angliae*) and perennial oat grass (*Chasmanthium latifolium*) in a mixed border planted for autumn color. These lily bulbs are best planted in spring.

When seeking to create color harmonies, it is vital to consider the relative heights of plants in addition to blooming time so that complementary colors occur in close proximity as well as in the same time frame. Here, several plants of the elegant white trumpet lily Crystal Palace, grown from bulbs, prove to be the perfect companion to tall ice-blue perennial delphiniums.

The edge of a driveway is made colorful with an assortment of flowering perennials, roses, and summer-flowering bulbs, including bulbous yellow-eyed grass (*Sisyrinchium striatum*), which is related to iris, and Turk's cap lilies. The border is raised by landscape ties to provide extra soil depth to a site that was scraped clear of top soil during house construction.

▲

A landscape that is planted with trees and shrubs displaying subtle foliage contrasts, unusual outlines, and interesting textures requires relatively few flowering plants for embellishment. Here, perennial pearly everlasting (*Anaphalis triplinervis*) lights up the landscape in a superb blending of trees and shrubs. In the background, a weeping form of blue Atlas cedar (*Cedrus atlantica* 'Glauca') creates an appealing curtain of evergreen beauty.

▼

Where a healthy old tree has been left by contractors, design garden spaces around it. Such trees not only add a lot of character to the property but offer ideal conditions for shade-loving plants, such as the yellow-flowered *Ligularia dentata* 'Desdemona', which displays magnificent dark-green heart-shaped leaves.

▲

To overcome a barren look, rock gardens demand a good selection of dwarf evergreens strategically placed among rock ledges. Featured in this alpine-style rock garden, coursed by a rocky stream, are weeping hemlock, spirelike Alberta spruce, and thread-leaf cypress. Low, spreading perennials such as pink dianthus, orange rock rose, and yellow sedum creep around boulders.

►

Abandoned quarries make fine rock gardens, for they create a cool, sheltered environment favoring verdant lawns and healthy growth of cool-season perennials, such as West Point lily-flowered tulips, seen here. The quarry walls are partially concealed by shrubby plants, including bushy evergreen rhododendrons, and also by evergreen English ivy and euonymus, which form green curtains from above.

▲

Roses, especially billowing shrub roses and rambling climbers, complement summer perennial plantings better than any other flowering shrub. Here, a climbing rose that has been allowed to spill informally into a section of lawn echoes the red in a mixed planting of false spiraea (*Astilbe × arendsii*) that edges a pool in the background.

▼

The best woodland gardens extend color into the tree canopy by means of flowering trees and shrubs. In this Connecticut spring garden, white and pink dogwoods thrust flowering branches skyward like a flock of butter-flies. In the understory, red azaleas provide another level of color, while the woodland floor sparkles with blue forget-me-nots (*Myosotis scorpioides*) and Jacob's ladder (*Polemonium reptans*), planted around a goldfish pond.

Though daylilies are a rather common summer-flowering perennial, new hybrids offer spectacular flower size and unusual bicolors and tricolors. Here, a large-flowered hybrid yellow daylily, Pleasure, and a tricolor, Right On, form an appealing color harmony with the blue evergreen needles and the deep blue of a Korean spruce.

▶

Perennial yellow loosestrife (*Lysimachia punctata*) forms a pool of dazzling light in a rock garden planted with dark foliage tones. Silvery Russian olive and bronze-leafed Thundercloud plum introduce appealing deciduous foliage colors, while evergreen blue spruce not only complements the yellow flowers but completes a tapestry of foliage hues that remains ornamental all season.

The rock garden at the New York Botanical Garden is one of the world's finest, not only because of its size but because it strikes exactly the right balance in its use of perennials, dwarf conifers, deciduous trees, rocks, and water in the overall design. Perennial ferns, Japanese primulas (*Primula japonica*), fringed bleeding heart (*Dicentra eximia*), and clumps of orange geum provide understated touches of color in spring.

Cushions of pink-flowering thyme bloom between flagstone stepping stones, while hardy Mediterranean pinks (*Saponaria ocymoides*) colonize a slope with soil held in place by stones. Yellow alyssum and heart-shaped leaves of *Epimedium versicolor* edge a flight of rustic steps, the complete design creating an appealing small-space rock garden.

Where a natural stream runs through a property, use it to make a naturalistic rock garden. The late H. Lincoln Foster, who wrote North America's most authoritative book on the subject, *Rock Gardening* (Timber Press), planted this rock garden along a spring-fed stream at the back of his Connecticut property. Varieties of mountain pinks decorate the upper rock shelves; yellow globe flower (*Trollius europaeus*) shines among a collection of native ferns.

Emulate an alpine scree (a mountain slope of small loose stones) in a small rock garden with a covering of gravel over the topsoil. In this garden, perennial alpine plants form low, compact cushions among boulders, while billowing, bushy plants, including a perennial *Acanthus mollis* with dark, glossy indented leaves, form an interesting backdrop. A silver-blue prostrate juniper helps create a transition between the shrubby background plants and the ground-hugging alpines.

Rock gardens in mountainous regions should use local stone and native plants to blend with the surrounding scenery, as at the Betty Ford Rock Garden in Vail, Colorado. Native mountain pinks spill over rock shelves, and the bare skeleton of a old juniper, which was dug from a nearby farm, adds a sculptural, wild beauty to the garden. Two kinds of broom—*Genista lydia* (center) and *Genista* 'Vancouver Gold' (right)—complement the perennial plantings.

Dry retaining walls not only help to provide garden spaces with privacy and shelter from the wind but can be crammed with a variety of alpine plants. Yellow perennial alyssum (*Aurinia saxatilis*) and white perennial candytuft (*Iberis sempervirens*) flower in early spring behind a teak bench at the Morris Arboretum, Philadelphia.

A flight of stone steps serves double duty as a series of terraces for housing a collection of small plants. The dwarf alpines growing here include peach-colored rock rose (*Helianthemum nummularium*), white *Rhodohypoxis baurii*, blue Siberian bellflower (*Campanula poscharskyana*), and yellow bush cinquefoil (*Potentilla fruticosa*).

Although the most colorful rock gardens need open, sunny locations and soils with excellent drainage, it is possible to produce a rock-garden effect in lightly shaded areas with boggy soil. At the edge of a pond, this rock garden uses perennial golden hakone grass (*Hakonechloa macra* 'Aureola') to cascade over boulders above a wild yellow-flowering *Mimulus* species. Iris and Japanese maple leaves add beautiful foliage contrasts.

Annual white sweet alyssum can be more than just an edging; when creatively planted, it can produce special effects. In this small rock garden, a foamlike quality is created by the planting of generous drifts of alyssum among hardy perennial thrift (*Armeria maritima*) and tender silvery blue perennial succulents, especially species of beadlike sedum, spiny agave, and rosettes of *Echeveria elegans.*

Perennial mosses are good ground-covers for shady areas. A distinctly Oriental appearance is created by the strategic placement of boulders and clumps of dwarf azaleas. Notice how the moss merges naturally into a grassy clearing, where brighter light allows fescue grasses to thrive.

Clusters of indigenous rock and exuberant perennial plantings achieve a wilderness look in the midst of a city. Within sight of the heavily congested George Washington Bridge in New York City, the rock garden at Wave Hill is a sanctuary of peace and tranquility. The perennials include white *Gaura lindheimeri*, silver plumes of eulalia grass (*Miscanthus sinensis*), and drifts of silvery snow-in-summer (*Cerastium tomentosum*).

Where large natural outcrops of rock occur on a property, it's a simple matter to clear away a strip of soil around the rock base to make a perennial border. The summer-flowering perennials in this coastal planting include pale yellow daylilies, peach-colored garden lilies, lemon coreopsis, purple loosestrife, and white shasta daisies.

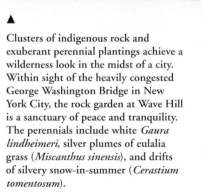

You can make a small-scale pond like this one by excavating a hole and lining the base with black plastic, held in place by the weight of water and, around the edges, by hefty rocks. Bright color comes from a hardy perennial waterlily and a pondside planting of false spiraea (*Astilbe* × *arendsii*). Perennial cattails (*Typha latifolia*), sedge grasses, yellow flag irises (*Iris pseudacorus*), and floating water clover (*Marsilea* species) add interesting foliage contrasts.

A detail of the floating perennial water plants in the pond above shows the beautiful foliage pattern achieved by the interplanting of a hardy waterlily, Escarboucle, with hardy water shamrock (*Marsilea quadrifolia*). Both are growing in submerged pots that control their aggressive tendencies.

In the southern states, a good way to decorate a large natural pond is to fill it with a combination of perennial lotus and perennial tropical waterlilies. The waterlilies float their large, round, mottled leaves on the surface, while the lotus project umbrellalike leaves aloft. Miscanthus grasses, cattails, and water irises line the edge.

A naturalistic pond provides a beautiful garden feature in summer, especially when it is easily seen from the house. This pond is located below the balcony of a master bedroom. Its center sparkles with wild white waterlilies, native to the Eastern Seaboard, while the pond margins glow with orange wayside daylilies. The spiky-leaved yellow flag iris have finished blooming.

Most formal water gardens use water plants growing in submerged tubs to maintain a clean-cut design. Here, at the Missouri Botanical Garden in St. Louis, many tender perennial aquatics are grown in tubs and taken indoors over winter. There are two kinds of cyperus (with umbrellalike leaves), crimson-flowering cannas, and a variegated hibiscus in the background.

The plants used in and around this bog garden produce a wild look. The banks of the stream are planted with perennial yellow flag irises (*Iris pseudacorus*) and pale blue biennial forget-me-nots (*Myosotis scorpioides*), which reseed themselves. A background of perennial ornamental grasses, a clump of hardy bamboo, and large, heart-shaped leaves of Japanese butterburr present a verdant background of naturalistic foliage textures.

This tiny water garden enjoys flowers all season by using water plants growing in pots and rotating them into the display when they bloom, in much the same way that some city gardeners do with window boxes. Beautiful peach-colored lotus blooms above a clump of blue African lily (*Agapanthus africanus*).

Miniature water gardens planted in large tubs are ideal for decorating a deck or patio. All the plants in this restful, cooling composition are submerged in small pots. In addition to two colors of hardy perennial waterlilies, the aquatic plants include silver water lettuce (*Pistia stratiotes*), a water canna, and a blue-green spiky rush (*Juncus* species).

A shady streamside rock garden can be planted entirely with spring-flowering perennial bulbs. The pendant orange bells of crown imperials (*Fritillaria imperialis*) rise above clumps of red Greigii hybrid tulips and yellow miniature daffodils. Evergreen gold-dust plant (*Aucuba japonica*), hardy to Zone 8, and a hardy juniper provide good textural contrasts in the background. White perennial wood anemone (*Anemone nemerosa*) spills into the stream in the foregound.

Give a water garden a colorful edging by planting a border around it. This border, surrounding a formal waterlily pool on three sides, has soil deep enough for sinking potted plants, so that several dramatic color changes are possible throughout the year. In autumn, perennial chrysanthemums are the featured pool edging.

Winter heliotrope (*Petasites fragrans*) is one of spring's earliest-flowering perennials. It is a bog-loving plant, and its beautiful, fragrant pink flowers are displayed on long stems before its large, heart-shaped leaves appear. Here, the elegant flower stems are seen striking through the sword-shaped leaves of flag iris and the ivy-shaped leaves of false spiraea (*Astilbe* x *arendsii*), which flower later.

Mid-Century Hybrid garden lilies are not only exquisite shade-loving perennials for early summer color but are sensational planted near a water feature, such as a stream or a waterlily pool, seen here in a woodland clearing.

Swimming pools are often an incongruous eyesore in gardens, but the owners of this New England property have skillfully used a naturalistic design to enhance the beauty of their rock garden. Spring perennials bloom among outcrops of rock, while island beds around the edges of the pool accommodate daylilies and garden lilies that flower later in the season.

Fragrance in a garden doesn't have to disappear when summer ends. In autumn, this garden features the sweet-scented white pendant flowers of a tender annual, *Nicotiana sylvestris*, and a large expanse of a hardy perennial variegated sage. Silvery perennial lavender cotton (*Santolina chamaecyparissus*) has a spicy fragrance. Tender perennial blue sage is grown as an annual wherever the ground freezes.

A wonderful addition to a stepping-stone path is cushions of pink creeping thyme (*Thymus serpyllum*) between the stones. When footsteps bruise the leaves, a pleasant aromatic fragrance is released into the air. This path extends down a slope at Oehme Gardens in Wenatchee, Washington.

Mollis hybrid azaleas and English bluebells (*Endymion nonscriptus*) are both exceedingly fragrant and enjoy lightly shaded locations. Here, along a woodland path, they are planted together in a dramatic blue-and-orange color harmony. Exbury hybrid azaleas—similar in appearance to the Mollis hybrids—are also highly fragrant, but Spanish bluebells (*Endymion hispanica*) are not.

Perhaps the most famous flower for fragrance in the garden is the rose, especially old garden rose varieties. In the rose garden at Lyndhurst Castle, Tarrytown, New York, roses are displayed in curved beds surrounding a beautiful Victorian-style gazebo; the high percentage of white roses echoes the color of the gazebo.

A delightful source of fragrance for a small garden (or pots) is scented-leaf geraniums, which surround this brick patio. Depending on the variety, they offer a potpourri of scents, including coconut, lemon, rose, orange, thyme, and peppermint. The flowers are small and sparse, so grow the plants for their foliage. Tender perennials, they can come indoors over winter in cold climates.

In the world of fragrances, the scent of perennial English lavender reigns supreme; it is used for soaps, perfumes, bath oils, and sachets. The flowers even make a refreshing aromatic tea. Here, the variety Munstead Blue is planted along terraced beds among silver and yellow flowering herbs, with a complementary background of blue junipers, themselves possessing a pleasant spicy fragrance.

Many drought-tolerant plants have fragrant flowers or foliage good for decorating slopes. Bordering a steep driveway in Santa Barbara, California, are yellow Jerusalem sage (center), yellow yarrow (right), and yellow lavender cotton. Blue French lavender (foreground) and a blue hybrid salvia, Allan Chittingham (background), complement the yellows and the silvery foliage tones.

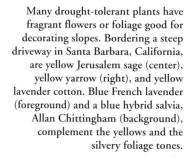

English lavender (*Lavandula angustifolia*) imparts such a well-liked fragrance that the owner of this garden has landscaped the side of a driveway with different varieties, forming cushions of mostly blue, pink, and white flowers. The lavender is interplanted with heather, which blooms earlier in the season. White and pink creeping thymes are used as an edging, pervading the air with a spicy fragrance whenever the wheels of a passing car crush the plants.

▲

Perennials for fresh-cut flowers need long stems, so in this old-fashioned garden, dwarf varieties are avoided. It includes blue balloon flower (*Platycodon grandiflora*), yellow yarrow (*Achillea*, also suitable for drying), pink and white summer phlox (*Phlox paniculata*), and red beebalm (*Monarda didyma*). At the left, pink and white annual cosmos, with feathery leaves, rise above this patch of perennials.

▼

Next to the vegetable garden is a good place to locate a cutting garden, since it is convenient to gather flowers for the house at the same time one is gathering food for the kitchen. This summer-flowering cutting garden features perennial white shasta daisies and orange butterfly weed (*Asclepias tuberosa*). Annual zinnias, marigolds, and statice are also included for cutting.

◄

Cutting flowers can spoil the garden display, but if enough flowers are planted, display gardens can do double duty as cutting gardens. This intensively planted, terraced cutting garden boasts a fine collection of perennial bearded iris, a mixture of perennial Iceland poppies (*Papaver nudicaule*), and biennial English foxgloves (*Digitalis* species). At the back is a row of crimson annual sweet peas that can fill a room with fragrance.

◄

Summer is the height of cut-flower season, but this old-fashioned garden has blooms to cut in spring. It features vigorous clumps of pink, white, and red herbaceous peonies, bicolored yellow-and-ginger bearded iris, blue and white Siberian iris, white sweet valerian (*Valeriana officinalis*), and a pink annual bachelor's button (*Centaurea cyanus*).

Cutting gardens need easy access. In author Derek Fell's cutting garden at Cedaridge Farm, Pennsylvania, a grid design of annuals is laid out in fifteen-foot rows, the total space evenly divided by a flagstone path. Edging the path are French marigolds, with annual sweet alyssum and perennial thyme forming mounds, like cushions of moss, between the cracks. Strategically placed perrennial plants - such as angel's trumpets and gladiolus - complement the annuals.

Cartwheel designs afford easy access to perennials for cutting. In this late-summer country garden, a gravel path encircles a central bed—the hub—and four curving beds form the wheel rim. The design uses a few annuals among bolder displays of perennial black-eyed Susans (*Rudbeckia hirta*), yellow goldenrod (*Solidago*), pink and white tuberous dahlias, and pink summer phlox (*Phlox paniculata*).

Because the cutting of flowers for arrangements can drastically deplete a display garden of blooms, some gardeners prefer to devote space to cut flowers in or alongside the vegetable garden, as shown here. In the foreground, a partial row of Asiatic hybrid lily Connecticut King is in full bloom, while the rest of the row features trumpet lilies, in bud. The scarecrow provides a whimsical decorative accent.

English lupines are outstanding additions to a formal cutting garden. Their tall flower spikes strike the sky like the spires of a citadel in this formal garden, which is designed in a grid of rectangular beds separated by grass paths and backed by a privet hedge. The pink lupines are good companions to clumps of blue Siberian iris. The unfolding buds of herbaceous peonies will soon add pompons of white, pink, and red to the garden.

Many of the plants grown in wild-flower gardens are rather small and delicate. But the American May apple (*Podophyllum peltatum*) offers a decided change of pace and evokes a wilderness aura in the landscape. Wild blue phlox

▶

(*Phlox divaricata*), yellow leopard's bane (*Doronicum cordatum*), and pink bleeding heart (*Dicentra spectabilis*) add splashes of color at ground level in this garden, while flowering dogwoods decorate the tree canopy above the white azaleas.

▶

If your property is wooded, thinning out the trees should enable you to grow a wide range of spring-flowering perennials. The owners of this New England property have retained a wooded look, but thinning has admitted sufficient light to grow not only grass but also sun-loving perennial alyssum (*Aurinia saxatilis*). The red azalea and blue forget-me-nots are naturally tolerant of shade.

▲

A garden's reputation can be established by rhododendrons alone. In this woodland setting, the filtered shade of tall sycamores provides exactly the right light conditions for a collection of rhododendrons, including a fragrant yellow Mollis hybrid azalea. An acid soil with high humus content works with the light shade to create spectacular growth and flowering.

▶

Though most spring-flowering bulbs will grow in full sun, light shade actually prolongs their bloom. An outcropping of moss-covered rocks in a grove of deciduous and evergreen trees provides a dramatic setting for a spring bulb garden planted with orange crown imperials, yellow daffodils, bicolored Greigii tulips, and blue Siberian squill (*Scilla siberica*).

The native American ostrich fern (*Matteucia struthiopteris*) can enliven a quiet woodland garden based on foliage. Here, its erect feathery fronds seem to explode with vitality in a serene woodland garden that relies heavily on foliage contrasts. Red azaleas, white Japanese andromeda, and pink and white flowering dogwoods help to carry color high above the woodland floor.

Not only are ponds attractive design elements for woodland gardens, but the pool of water creates a clearing with sufficient light for flowering plants to grow around the margin. The colorful perennials in this pond-side planting include red *Astilbe* x *arendsii*, pink *Filipendulina rubra*, and yellow *Mimulus aurantiacus*. All tolerate light shade and boggy soil.

Where streams flow through woodland gardens, cutting a notch in the tree canopy will allow the sun to shine through to make the running water glitter and sparkle. This boggy woodland garden is heavily planted with Siberian and Japanese irises that will bloom later in the season, but here, orange candelabra primroses shimmer along the stream bank in early spring.

Carpet a woodland garden with native American wildflowers, such as the white foamflower (*Tiarella cordifolia*) and the two shades of wild blue phlox (*Phlox divaricata*) seen in this garden. A blue wisteria vine and a pink Japanese azalea help to extend color into the tree canopy.

In a deeply shaded area, ferns, hostas, and periwinkle foliage (*Vinca minor*) create a romantic mood around a frog pond. Where the natural woodland canopy thins out, sufficient light allows azaleas and dogwoods to flaunt pink and white blossoms like flights of butterflies.

When planting this woodland garden in upstate New York, the owners wanted floral color they could view from the house. After the azalea shrubs below the window have finished flowering, they are kept low by pruning that maintains a vista into woodland, where rhododendrons flower beneath the light shade of tall native maples.

The bronze foliage of a Thundercloud plum in this woodland garden helps to break up the monotony of the greens that tend to dominate a wooded landscape. Bronze leaf coloring also provides a good contrast for the spires of English foxgloves, which tolerate light shade.

A woodland glade does not need a lot of different plants to look enchanting. Here, in Southern California, flowers of *Clivia miniata*, a tender perennial bulb, shine among the shadows. Its straplike leaves also contrast well with the tender banana plants in the background. Often classified as trees, bananas are true perennials. The mother plant dies after flowering, but a new generation survives from its rhizomes.

Consider native plant species for carefree meadow plantings. In midsummer, this New England meadow sparkles with color from purple loosestrife (*Lythrum salicaria*), yellow goldenrod (*Solidago* species), and common cattails (*Typha latifolia*). All are indigenous to the area and tolerate boggy soil. The loosestrife and cattails define the course of a small stream.

Though lupines are native to North America, it took the British to create beautiful color mixtures, such as these Russell hybrids. They are naturalized in a Long Island, New York, garden, blooming in spring when the nights are cool and whenever coastal breezes provide mild conditions.

The three Texas wildflowers in this meadow planting all thrive in alkaline soil: annual Texas bluebonnets (*Lupinus texensis*), perennial orange Indian paintbrush (*Castilleja* species), and perennial pink wine cups (*Oeno-thera speciosa*). Though the blue-bonnets and paintbrush are difficult to establish in northern states with harsh winters, the wine cups are a hardy perennial that thrive coast-to-coast.

Japanese candelabra primulas (*Primula japonica*) thrive in moist, boggy soil along the edges of streams. To create this mass planting between a sunlit meadow and a shady woodland, the owner erected low dams at intervals along the stream and, at each dam site, set a sprinkler so that the plants can be watered during summer when the stream dries up.

To make the most of a sloping meadow, consider creating an arrangement of rocky waterfalls, designed to look entirely natural, like these in an alpine meadow at Oehme Gardens in Washington. Clumps of native mosses and ferns thrive close to the sparkling water, while drought-tolerant sedums and thyme spread across the sunny slope in great sweeps of yellow, pink, and white.

For a meadow garden with stronger color tones than might be possible with the use of true indigenous species, consider using garden varieties developed by nursery people from native American wildflowers, like white and red beebalm (*Monarda didyma*), yellow black-eyed Susans (*Rudbeckia hirta*), yellow false sunflower (*Heliopsis scabra*), and white foxglove penstemon (*Penstemon digitalis*).

Many meadows have soft, low spots where water does not drain freely; stepping stones can help people traverse a swampy area in comfort. Clumps of perennial ornamental grasses create a transition between the low, boggy lake margin, where yellow flag iris and blue Siberian iris grow spectacularly.

Wildflower meadows need not be a kaleidoscope of varieties and colors to look beautiful. This cliff-top meadow near Newport, Rhode Island, was seeded the previous year with two hardy perennials: white shasta daisies (*Leucanthemum* x *superbum*) and yellow plains coreopsis (*Coreopsis grandiflora*). Peak flowering occurs in midsummer.

No other flower among hardy perennials can match the color impact of modern hybrid daylilies in mid-summer. The owners of this meadow planting not only collect daylily varieties and display them in sunny beds around their property but divide up thick clumps and sell them as a cottage industry.

Lavender blooms continuously from early summer to autumn frosts, and it thrives even in impoverished soil, provided it has excellent drainage. Here, clumps of hardy English lavender have been planted throughout an olive orchard to establish long-lasting beauty and fragrance.

Mule's ears (*Wyethia amplexicaulis*) are a perennial sunflower native to the Pacific Northwest. They tolerate light shade and are especially effective planted in woodland clearings with white mountain phlox (as seen here), or among orchard trees. Blooming in spring, in the Northwest they are one of the first plants to populate scorched earth.

Cheerful trumpet daffodils are one of the most welcome harbingers of spring. To be maintained in a meadow planting like this, they need feeding twice a year: in autumn after frost, and again in spring before the plants bloom. Also, the tops must not be cut until eight weeks after the flowers have faded.

▼

Most desert perennials bloom in April and May, following the winter rains. At the Desert Botanical Garden near Phoenix, Arizona, desert plants from all over the world are displayed in beds raised above caliche (an impervious, concrete-hard subsoil) by boulders. Here, the colorful blooms of orange-flowered Mexican shrimp plant (*Justica spicigera*) and desert penstemon (*Penstemon parryi*) flower together in early spring.

▶

A desert garden can be more than just cactus. Drought tolerant desert wildflowers add bursts of color during their blooming season. This informal border, which edges a path, features purple sand verbena (*Verbena rigida*) and pink showy penstemon (*Penstemon spectabilis*).

◀

In a dry climate, use drought-tolerant plants to cover a slope. Here, at the University of California at Berkeley, annual South African daisies (*Dimorphotheca* species), perennial bulbs, and perennial succulents carpet a hillside. Orange ixias and yellow sparaxis, tender spring-flowering bulbs resembling freesias, are blooming with orange and red aloes.

▲

A beautiful bicolored selection of a South African ice plant (*Lampranthus aureus*) makes an ideal edging for a path in a desert garden and blooms in early spring. This tender perennial complements the blue sedum (*Pachyveri glauca*) and the orange-flowering *Aloe vera* (behind). Edging the opposite side of the path is rosy ice plant (*Drosanthemum roseum*). All are drought tolerant.

▼

Use garden structures that blend well with the environment to decorate spaces featuring desert plants. In this Tucson, Arizona, garden a border of mixed perennials—all native to the Sonoran Desert—forms a semicircle around a curved adobe wall fitted with a slatted wooden bench. Flowering sand verbena (*Abronia villosa*) and scarlet bugler (*Penstemon centranthifolius*) are shown in the foreground.

▶

In desert areas it's possible to landscape beautiful gardens by using only indigenous species, like this native plant garden at the Sonora Desert Museum near Tucson. Indeed, the entire property contains plants found only in the Sonoran Desert. Candelabralike teddy bear cholla and prickly barrel cactus are true perennial cacti. Clumps of yellow goldfields (*Lasthenia chrysostoma*) are annuals. Silvery jojoba bush—the source of jojoba oil—and the sinuous limbs of an ocotillo cactus add foliage and structural interest to the background.

◀

The sculptural shapes of cacti can be combined in dramatic ways, especially near contemporary-style architecture. Here, at the Huntington Botanical Garden in Los Angeles, cacti and succulents are grouped to create beautiful structural and textural contrasts. With the pink blossoms of a silk floss tree as a background, the diverse shapes of a spiny golden barrel cactus, a nubby green cereus cactus, and a silvery old man cactus display a bizarre, artistic beauty.

▲

Coastal California gardeners can draw on the especially rich plant palette of South Africa. The botanical garden of the University of California at Irvine displays its extensive collection of drought-tolerant South African perennial desert succulents in landscape settings. In early spring, the bright orange flower clusters of *Aloe striata* complement the brilliant yellow blossoms of *Senecio praecox*.

Plantings of drought-resistant perennials can turn a hillside into a garden and can help prevent erosion during seasonal rains. On this California slope, silvery mounds of lavender cotton (*Santolina chamaecyparissus*) sparkle with buttonlike yellow flowers. They are complemented by mounds of English and French lavender, and by clouds of blue *Salvia* 'Allan Chittingham'. Scented-leaf geraniums and white Mermaid roses spill from a balcony.

Few perennials are as drought tolerant as tender perennial cape marigold (*Arctotheca calendula*), used here to carpet a slope in a residential section of San Diego. Cape marigold flowers in early summer, and its silvery green foliage stays decorative all year, knitting together in a tight weave to control soil erosion on sunny slopes.

The drought-tolerant perennial in the foreground of this garden, *Osteospermum ecklonis* 'Blue Streak', presents a mass of color even when the flowers close up on cloudy days. The daisylike flowers are white or pink on top and deep purple underneath. Annual sweet alyssum (*Lobularia maritima*), a good companion, blooms in the background.

Pink-flowering weeping lantana (*Lantana montevidensis*) is a tender evergreen perennial vine, excellent for controlling soil erosion in mild-winter areas of California and the South. It hugs the ground with its long, trailing stems, flowers continuously, and makes a good companion for ivy-leaf geraniums, which are everblooming in warm climates.

A lightly shaded hillside is a perfect place to grow spring-flowering bulbs such as tulips. Here, at Minter Gardens in Chilliwack, British Columbia, drifts of Darwin hybrid tulips descend a slope. In the background, clumps of perennial blue columbine (*Aquilegia vulgaris*) create a misty appearance.

Drought-tolerant perennial ornamental grasses and New Zealand flax can be planted to control the erosion of sandy coastal soil and are excellent plants for dry seaside gardens on the West Coast. They also paint the landscape in green and amber tones. The picnic table rests on variegated St. Augustine grass (*Stenotaphrum secondatum* 'Variegatum'). Deer grass (*Muhlenbergia rigens*), in the foreground, and fountain grasses (*Pennisetum* species), in the rear, add textural and color variations. Though these are tender varieties, hardy substitutes are available for eastern gardens.

Drifts of hardy perennial mountain pinks (*Phlox subulata*) create a wild-flower meadow in a Connecticut garden. Interplanted among the phlox—for later flowering—are clumps of dwarf iris. Though mountain phlox include vibrant pinks and reds, this planting uses mostly white and shades of blue to echo the siding on the house.

It sometimes takes only one plant species to make the most of a difficult site. Here, a mass planting of African lily (*Agapanthus africanus*) thrives not only on a steep slope, but also in impoverished sandy soil, exposed to glaring sun, frequent winds, and dousings of salt spray. African lily grows best in a Mediterranean climate, such as coastal California.

▲

Many kinds of ornamental grasses enjoy coastal conditions, including natal grass (*Rychelytrum repans*), which produces shimmering light pink flower heads in autumn. Though tender, and sensitive to winterkill where the ground freezes, natal grass is a striking accent in California coastal gardens, where it tolerates impoverished soil and salt spray.

▼

The yellow lupine (*Lupinus arborea*) in this cliff-top planting is native to the Pacific Northwest, and it looks sensational planted alone to naturalize freely. Here, overlooking the Pacific Ocean near Carmel, California, it complements a colorful collection of tough, salt-tolerant Mediterranean and South African perennials, including pride of Madeira (*Echium fastuosum*), sea lavender, an orange perennial gazania, and hardy silvery lavender cotton.

▲

Footpaths leading down to a beach through sand dunes are good places to consider borders of salt-tolerant flowering perennials, such as ivy-leaf geraniums (*Pelargonium peltatum*) and blue kingfisher daisies (*Felicia amelloides*). These are tender perennials that will overwinter in coastal California and may be grown as annuals in other coastal areas.

◀

South African daisies and ice plants are famous for their love of coastal conditions. In this coastal California garden, tender *Drosanthemum roseum* (rosy ice plant) extends like a carpet down the slope. Also present are patches of yellow-flowering hottentot fig (*Carpobrotus edulis*), an ice plant with red-tipped, succulent foliage, and white trailing African daisy (*Osteospermum fruticosum*).

Lilies are not generally regarded as perennials suitable for coastal gardens, but along a windswept cliff-top near Gloucester, Massachusetts, here's proof that the orange tiger lily (*Lilium lancifolium*) can thrive almost to the water's edge. It is shown in company with the orange-scarlet fruits of a rugosa rose and the fernlike foliage of young sumac trees. The small black bulblets that form in the leaf axils of the lilies readily sprout in moist, well-drained soil and establish new colonies.

In this verdant coastal garden overlooking Monterey Bay, California, the location of the house, plus salt-tolerant and wind-resistant shrubs, helps to shelter delicate flowering plants. A mixture of spring-flowering annuals and perennials crowds the edges of a serpentine brick walk, which defines a beautiful freeform turf lawn. A moongate leads to a wildflower meadow planted with African daisies.

Autumn-flowering perennials for coastal gardens are scarce, but colonies of naked ladies (*Amaryllis belladonna*) flower spectacularly in mild coastal areas, such as coastal California. Though they are tender, there is a related hardy summer-flowering species (*Lycoris squamigera*) that will overwinter in the Northeast. Both are grown from bulbs.

This colorful perennial garden is sandwiched between a freshwater pond and the wild Atlantic Ocean in a Long Island, New York, coastal community. The floral color is established by clumps of pink chrysanthemums, yellow black-eyed Susans, red Dragon's-blood sedum, pink Autumn Joy sedum, and crimson rose mallow (*Hibiscus moscheutos*). Tussocks of ornamental grasses and dwarf evergreens provide foliage contrasts.

Chapter Five

Seasonal Changes

*U*nlike many flowering annuals, which may bloom continuously through three seasons, most perennials planted in North America have a particular season of bloom, sometimes lasting just two or three weeks. The best two months for perennial color are June and September, which are relatively cool months over most sections of North America. The perennial season can be said to begin and end with a big bang—daffodils in April and chrysanthemums in October—though there are a few interesting perennials that will bloom ahead of daffodils and a few others that will soldier on after chrysanthemums have faded. This chapter shows some of the seasonal highlights.

Winter

Most perennials go dormant in winter. They lose their leaves and survive winter freezes by means of underground bulbs or fleshy roots. Though nodding white snowdrops and cheerful yellow aconites may brave the cold to bloom in February, it is the month of March that really starts to set the floral world in motion. Consider establishing a "March walk," a special section of your garden where March-blooming perennials can be admired in a group.

Several kinds of winter-blooming heathers, particularly pink and white selections of Scots heather (*Calluna vulgaris*), are good for establishing generous sweeps of color. They especially like sunny slopes and a humus-rich soil. The variety Blaze Away has flaming orange foliage all through the winter months.

There are many early-flowering minor bulbs that will bloom even before the last snowfall. Frequently, they will bloom during a brief warming spell, to be covered over in the night by snow, giving the impression of blooming through the snow.

In frost-free areas, gardeners can enjoy the early flowering of many tender perennial bulbs, especially Persian buttercups (*Ranunculus asiaticus*), French anemones (*Anemone coronaria*), and calla lilies (*Zantedeschia aethiopica*). Also invaluable for gardens in mild-winter areas are many forms of flowering aloe (especially the orange *Aloe saponaria* and the scarlet *Aloe arborescens*) and small, tender-perennial shrubs, such as Japanese camellia (*Camellia japonica*).

Until the main tulip displays provide vibrant reds and flaming oranges, the best winter color harmonies tend to be subdued, mostly pastel bicolor and triad combinations, using yellow with shades of blue, plus white. Early daffodils (such as February Gold), crocuses, and forsythia provide strong yellows in the late winter–early spring landscape; grape hyacinths, crocuses, snow irises, Siberian squill, and snow glories all provide strong blues. White snowdrops and yellow aconites are a sparkling yellow-and-white combination, especially against a background of dried brown leaves or pine needles.

Used alone, the winter-flowering Lenten rose may look rather drab, but if it is planted beneath the branches of a Korean azalea, lovely lavender petals from the azalea will carpet the ground like confetti to give the Lenten rose a colorful background. A nearby planting of yellow-twig dogwood and red-twig dogwood, deciduous shrubs with colorful, erect stems, will also complement Lenten roses. Not only does *Mahonia bealii* have lustrous, hollylike evergreen foliage that is a good contrast with Lenten roses, but also it has dusky, blue-black berry clusters that light up a bleak, wintery landscape.

Place blue Siberian squill beneath the branches of a saucer magnolia (*Magnolia soulangiana*), and chances are the squill will bloom at the same time to complement the light pink magnolia petals, and to harmonize with them when the petals fall.

Spring

Trumpet daffodils and hybrid tulips command such a strong presence in the landscape that it's possible to have a satisfying early-spring garden using varieties almost exclusively from these two plant families.

Several outstanding biennials make good companions to daffodils and tulips, particularly blue forget-me-nots, pink and red English daisies, yellow and orange Siberian wallflowers, and purple money plant. A wealth of hardy perennials also surges into bloom at the first sign of a warming trend. The best for color impact include low, spreading mountain phlox, various species of columbine, several kinds of bleeding heart, blue phlox, blue bugle weed, sparkling white foamflower, cheerful violets (especially the precocious yellow-and-maroon bicolor *Viola* known as Johnny-jump-up), yellow perennial alyssum, dazzling white perennial candytuft, and a multitude of hardy primroses. Over most sections of North America, the first week of May is considered the time of "peak bloom" for perennial color. With azaleas and dogwoods to carry color up into the sky, perennial gardens can be a riot of color. Since 80 percent of hardy perennials are said to bloom in a one-month period, spanning April and May, the big challenge is to maintain enough good color through the end of May until early June, when dramatic color harmonies can be orchestrated with bearded iris, herbaceous peonies, and roses. Siberian iris (*Iris sibirica*), Russell hybrid lupine (*Lupinus polyphyllum*), ox-eye daisy (*Leucanthemum vulgare*), tree peony (*Paeonia suffruticosa*), and English foxglove (*Digitalis purpurea*) will meet the challenge, especially supported by a few choice hardy hybrid rhododendrons, such as Scintillation and Roseum Elegans.

Some often-overlooked perennials for spring color include the yellow leopard's bane (*Doronicum caucasicum*), Spanish bluebells (*Endymion hispanica*), thrift (*Armeria maritima*), false indigo (*Baptisia australis*), blue stars (*Amsonia tabernaemontana*), and various kinds of ornamental onion (alliums), particularly the white *Allium neapolitanum*, a good companion to Spanish bluebells.

In frost-free locations, many kinds of South African daisies produce spectacular spring color, particularly perennial forms of gazania (*Gazania rigens leucolana*) and shimmering ice plants (notably *Lampranthus* species). Whole hillsides can be planted with the trailing African daisy (*Osteospermum fruticosum*) in pink or white, as well as the pink weeping lantana (*Lantana montevidensis*). The drought-tolerant matilija poppy (*Romneya coulteri*) is especially good for cool coastal areas, covering itself with beautiful white flowers up to eight inches across, each flower highlighted by a bright golden yellow mound of stamens. Angel's trumpets (*Brugmansia* species), particularly the white, have always been popular woody plants for adding tall highlights to spring perennial gardens. There are also pink and yellow forms, but by far the most free-flowering is a hybrid, Charles Grimaldi, which covers itself several times a year with masses of highly fragrant, golden yellow blooms up to eighteen inches long.

Good color harmonies for spring are yellow and white (yellow basket-of-gold and white candytuft, for example), blue and white (blue *Iris reticulata* and white *Anemone blanda*), and red and yellow (red Emperor tulips and King Alfred daffodils).

Summer

For perennial plants, the biggest bane of summer over most of North America is mildew disease. Summer phlox and beebalm (*Monarda didyma*) are especially susceptible to it. Left unchecked, the disease discolors leaves, first coating them with a powdery white fungus, then turning them an ugly brown. Flowering performance is poor, and the ornamental value of the plants is ruined. Though fungicidal sprays can keep the disease at bay, it pays to consider disease-resistant varieties.

Many popular European perennials, such as delphiniums and carnations, don't like North America's hot summers. With adequate irrigation, they can often soldier on through hot days, providing there is a cool respite at night, but when nights also turn uncomfortably hot, they are doomed. Not so those perennials developed from native wildflowers. Butterfly weed (*Asclepias tuberosa*), rose mallow (*Hibiscus moscheutos*), purple coneflower (*Echinacea purpurea*), gayfeather (*Liatris* species), and other Americans all relish the sun and warmth. Unfortunately, the selection of heat-tolerant plants is not as extensive as that of cool-season perennials, so the best perennial gardens tend to feature lots of heat-tolerant annuals, particularly those with the ability to bloom a long time, such as gloriosa daisies, French marigolds, and mildew-resistant zinnias for sunny spots, and impatiens, begonias, and coleus for shady places.

Pink and blue make an especially pleasant "cooling" color harmony for summer, such as in a combination of pink summer phlox and pink Fairy roses with blue Russian sage and blue globe thistle. A bolder color harmony for summer is red, green, and silver, such as red beebalm, green scented-leaf geranium foliage, and silvery lamb's ears.

Autumn

In those sections of North America with snow cover in winter, autumn can be the most colorful time of year. The color comes not only from late-blooming perennials, such as asters, chrysanthemums, and maiden grasses, but also from the leaf colors of certain perennials. Many ornamental grasses (such as Japanese bloodgrass) and hostas (such as Autumn Glow) have striking fall foliage colors.

Consider also the changing leaf colors of deciduous trees and shrubs that provide dramatic background contrasts. For example, contrasting the blues of Siberian asters with the golden yellows of tulip poplars can create one of the most refreshing color harmonies of autumn: orange and blue. Another striking autumnal color harmony is the contrast of yellow and red, such as yellow cushion chrysanthemums and red burning-bush foliage, or the rusty red flowers of *Sedum* 'Autumn Joy' with beige-colored fountain grass.

Without doubt, the most treasured small tree for autumn color is the Japanese maple. Its slow growth and low, spreading, mounded habit make it ideal for placement as an accent in rock gardens and mixed perennial borders to provide sensational autumn color—yellow, orange, or red, depending on the variety.

▼

Crocus are easily naturalized under trees casting light shade, and they bloom, even in the midst of turf grass, a week or two before the earliest daffodils. One of the most appealing varieties is the bicolored Pickwick, which is white-petaled with purple veins. Here, it creates an eye-catching contrast among dried brown leaves and yellow daffodil foliage.

▲

Yellow winter aconites (*Eranthis hyemalis*) and white snowdrops (*Galanthus nivalis*) are a pretty combination for an early-spring woodland garden. Even in the Northeast, they may bloom as early as February, during a brief, bright warming spell. In a humus-rich soil, kept free of weeds during summer, both will seed themselves and naturalize freely.

►

A sure sign that winter has finally loosened its grip on the garden is the blooming of daffodils, which are especially nice when naturalized beneath the outstretched flowering branches of a white star magnolia (*Magnolia stellata*), as seen here. This vigorous variety, Carlton, is especially good for naturalizing because its yellow petals and gold trumpet stand out even under cloudy skies.

▲
Daffodils and tulips can provide color
from mid-April through mid-May.
Select early, mid-season, and late
varieties for a succession of color.

►
A dry stone retaining wall is an ideal
spot for mixing early-spring-flowering
perennials with tulips. Cascading
down the wall like a curtain are pink
false rock cress (*Aubrieta deltoidia*),
yellow perennial alyssum (*Aurinia
saxatilis*), and white perennial
candytuft (*Iberis sempervirens*).
The yellow tulips help carry color
into a shrub border, where an
early rhododendron has started
to flower.

▲
Bring color to a slope with informal
plantings of spring-flowering bulbs
between shrubs. Here, a clump of
crown imperial (*Fritillaria imperialis*)
contrasts its bright green leaves and
orange bell-shaped flowers with the
pale yellow flowers of a Warminster
broom (*Cytisus* × *praecox*) and a blue
holly (*Ilex* × *meserve*). White daffodils
sparkle in the distance, and blue grape
hyacinths rim a circular lawn.

Pink, white, and blue create an appealing color harmony for spring. Peak bloom in this New England woodland garden is in the first week of May, when the brilliance of white-flowering native dogwoods combines with the blizzard of pink blooms of native and hybrid azaleas. Carpeting the woodland floor are pools of blue forget-me-nots and strings of pink bleeding heart.

If you live in the woods, take advantage of early-spring sunlight to grow an assortment of cool-season perennials that bloom before the overhead trees fully leaf out. In this garden, clumps of blue crested iris (*Iris cristata*), blue forget-me-nots (*Myosotis scorpioides*), and pink creeping phlox (*Phlox stolonifera*) form colorful cushions among gray boulders that help to tie the design together. Dwarf conifers provide structural accents.

Use containers to try some offbeat planting schemes. Where most people might use pansies or violas for a spring display, this pedestal planter (actually a birdbath) is filled with *Rhodohypoxis baurii*, a tender bulbous perennial from South Africa. Where winter freezing occurs, overwinter the plant, like gladiolus, by lifting the bulbs and storing them indoors.

Spring gardens tend to be full of pastels, but here is a bolder combination for a warm climate. This colorful spring border contrasts red and blue French anemones (*Anemone coronaria*) and white marguerite daisies (*Argyranthemum frutescens*) with a splash of yellow from Crystal Bowl hybrid pansies, which are noted for clear colors without dark blotches.

Many native American wildflowers are a good source of spring color. Along a woodland path, blue phlox (*Phlox divaricata*), blue Jacob's ladder (*Polemonium caeruleum*), wild blue violets (*Viola odorata*), and wild red columbine (*Aquilegia canadensis*)—all North American natives—are in good company with yellow leopard's bane (*Doronicum cordatum*), blue forget-me-nots (*Mysotis scorpioides*), and white perennial candytuft (*Iberis sempervirens*).

A beautiful stand of tulip poplars (*Liriodendron tulipifera*) rises above a valley coursed by a stream. The fast-growing native American trees cast light shade, creating a perfect environment for azaleas and a rich green carpet of groundcovers, including periwinkle, hostas, ferns, pachysandra, and English ivy.

Perennial borders sometimes need a distinct separation from one garden space to another, such as this trellis-work fence between a woodland garden and a sunny perennial border that mixes biennials and perennials. In the foreground, perennial pink *Geranium endressii* contrasts with biennial blue Canterbury bells and spires of blue delphiniums. Further along, red and pink biennial sweet Williams contrast with yellow perennial sundrops.

▼

Warm climates do not generally foster the growth of English cottage-garden flowers. But you may find that, although your summers are hot and dry, your area enjoys cool spring seasons that are perfect for the flowering of at least one cottage-garden favorite: biennial English foxgloves (*Digitalis purpurea*). Here, in California, foxgloves bloom in an old olive grove that also provides adequate shade for azaleas.

▼

Camellias are the earliest flowering shrubs for mild-climate areas. Though they are popular planted along house foundations in many southern and Pacific coastal areas, they are at their best in the light shade of deciduous trees, as seen here. Baby's tears serves as an easy-care substitute for moss along the stepping-stone path in this Japanese garden.

▲

Antique garden roses are the perfect ending to a parade of spring color. Here, Seven Sisters climbing rose flaunts masses of deep pink blooms over an arched trellis, which shelters a secluded bench that faces a semicircle of old shrub roses.

▶

The addition of annuals makes it easier to maintain a colorful flower border through summer. Though this border features perennial red beebalm (*Monarda didyma*), blue Russian sage (*Perovskia atriplicifolia*), and lavender *Agastache hyssopus* as tall highlights, it is the snappy colors of cherry red zinnias, yellow marigolds, crimson prince's feather, and pink wax begonias that make the planting shine.

◀

For early summer color, few plants can rival perennial hollyhocks. Though many gardeners prefer the old-fashioned single-flowered kinds— their tapering spikes studded with hibiscuslike blossoms—the double kinds, with their fluffy pompons, should not be overlooked. This variety, Powderpuffs, will flower the first year from seed started early indoors eight to ten weeks before outdoor planting.

◀

Another beautiful combination of annuals and perennials keeps these island beds colorful. The center of attraction of this group of beds is perennial *Coreopsis grandiflora*, which echoes the yellow of hybrid hibiscus flowers and golden evergreen euonymus leaves in the background. Drifts of white annual sweet alyssum help unite the beds.

Gertrude Jekyll liked to capitalize on the strong yellows of summer perennials, saying that a yellow garden was like a splash of sunshine on a cloudy day. Though this sunny border features a few annuals (Chippendale zinnia, scarlet sage, and orange cosmos, for example), its brightness comes from *Coreopsis tinctoria* (foreground), *Rudbeckia hirta* (center), and yellow hybrid daylilies (rear). Silver lamb's ears is used as an edging, and white *Physostegia virginiana* is a background highlight.

The presence of water has a cooling influence on summer days. This simple rectangular waterlily pool is positioned at the edge of a patio, with a beautiful lawn vista beyond. Though the pool is formal, its angular design is softened by a cluster of foliage plants and hanging baskets surrounding a eucalyptus tree, and by the free-form border edging the lawn in the background.

If a sophisticated, classical perennial garden is what you're after, seek subtle foliage contrasts and subdued color, and avoid using too many annuals. This elegant double border features a connoisseur's collection of perennials and a fine templelike structure as a focal point.

For summer borders, choose varieties of summer phlox with care because they are notoriously susceptible to mildew disease, which badly discolors their foliage. One mildew-resistant variety is Eva Cullum, seen here, whose deep pink flowers present a magnificent contrast with the glowing yellow, daisylike flowers of *Helianthus* x *multiflorus.*

▶

Surround a brick patio with ornamental grasses for seclusion. In grass expert Kurt Bluemel's garden, a clump of *Miscanthus sinensis* 'Gracillimus' provides not only privacy, but also a good foliage contrast with a prostrate form of cut-leaf Japanese maple in the foreground. Tender Burgundy Giant fountain grass decorates a wooden planter in the background.

▼

Wide-open spaces sometimes call for large plants. This late summer display, bordering a stream, gleams with yellow black-eyed Susans and orange sneeze-weed (*Helenium autumnale*). The arching leaf blades of *Miscanthus sinensis* 'Gracillimus' contrast with the erect swordlike leaves of Japanese iris. Hardy white swamp hibiscus (*Hibiscus palustris*) and pink Joe-pye weed tolerate boggy soil.

▲

A simple but beautiful monochromatic pink design uses double-flowered Pink Powderpuffs hollyhocks (*Alcea rosea*) behind a mass of Bright Star purple coneflower (*Echinacea purpurea*), a vigorous variety with extra-large flowers that may measure up to five inches across.

▲

Where summers are hot and humid, many perennials will sulk unless the soil is kept cool. The proximity of a flagstone path cools these curving perennial borders. The use of an organic mulch (bark chips) further helps to keep the soil comfortably cool for the superior blooming of white feverfew (*Chrysanthemum parthenium*) and yellow lady's mantle (*Alchemilla vulgaris*).

▲

Tender perennial angel's trumpet (*Brugmansia* 'Charles Grimaldi') flowers several times a year and makes a dramatic tropical highlight for late-summer cutting gardens. Gardeners who do not live in frost-free climates can grow angel's trumpet in tubs. Move them indoors before frost, withhold water, and let the woody plants winter over in a dormant state.

▶

Wherever garden lilies (*Lilium* hybrids) do well, daylilies (*Hemerocallis* hybrids) should make a fine succession planting. This freeform swimming pool features island beds filled with summer-flowering Enchantment garden lilies, presaging a glorious daylily display that will begin several weeks later. A fine collection of dwarf conifers rises along the terraces. Blue junipers echo the color of the water.

◄

By choosing varieties carefully, it's possible to have daylilies blooming from June through October, though peak flowering occurs in August. The removal of spent blooms prolongs the display. Here, a mass of summer-flowering daylilies encircles an evergreen white pine at the edge of a lawn.

▼

A highly formal layout of straight paths and rectangular beds may look too severe; soften it by hiding the edges with perennials that spill into the gravel paths. Here, a dwarf mullein (*Verbascum chaixii*) produces a beautiful clump of lustrous green leaves and spires of yellow flowers that stab the sky like rockets.

For a summer planting of hot colors, try combining rosy red valerian (*Centranthus ruber*) and orange and yellow dog fennel *Anthemis sancti-johannis,* as seen here in Claude Monet's garden at Giverny, France. These early-summer perennials cover the withered leaves of Oriental poppies, which bloom at the same time as bearded iris, whose sword-shaped leaves are still visible as a decorative edging.

▶

Plume poppy (*Macleaya cordata*) is a vigorous plant with long-lasting buff-colored flower plumes that turn pink as the autumn season advances. Though not easy to use in small, confined spaces, it makes a good tall highlight along high fences and walls and as a background for mixed perennial borders.

After the first frosts of autumn, the color of leaves can maintain vibrancy in a garden. Grape leaves turn golden as the vines wither; here, draped over an arbor, they create a tunnel of russet tones along a flagstone path, and they contrast effectively with the silvery leaves of lamb's ears (*Stachys byzantina*) tumbling over a retaining wall.

A garden without benches is like a theater without seats. Choose benches that are good to look at and comfortable, placed so they also offer a beautiful view. This curving perennial border is actually the terminus of a lawn vista, the ornate bench offering a fine view back toward the house along the facing freeform beds. Dahlias have just started their autumn display.

A magnificent autumn composition plays the tousled leaf blades and reddish flower plumes of silvery eulalia grass (*Miscanthus sinensis* 'Variegatus') against the rusty red flower clusters of *Sedum* 'Autumn Joy', purple New England asters, and silvery green *Artemisia* 'Silver King'.

Without a flower in sight, a beautiful composition of fall foliage effects can be achieved in a small city garden with a balance of evergreen shrubs, a berry-bearing *Viburnum dilatatum*, and hardy perennials with strong foliage contrasts, including broad-leafed hostas, spiky yuccas, and tussocks of grasslike Siberian iris.

Gardeners pressed for space can pack plenty of fall color into a confined area. Here, a patio planter with dwindling spires of blue *Veronica spicata* gives way to tiers of autumn color from dwarf blue *Aster* 'Professor Kippenberg', dwarf yellow goldenrod (*Solidago* 'Peter Pan'), glittering red flower clusters of *Panicum virgatum* 'Heavy Metal', and shimmering plumes of *Miscanthus sinensis* 'Silver Feather'.

Pacific chrysanthemum (*Ajania pacifica*) is the last hardy perennial to bloom outdoors in the Northeast. For most of the year, it has decorative indented leaves, each with a distinct white margin. The plant remains low and compact until autumn, when the stems elongate to produce clusters of yellow buttonlike flowers—a mass of unexpected color when most other plants have been browned by frost.

Dinnerplate dahlias, tender perennial bulbs that must be lifted after the tops die down, continue flowering until fall frost. This orange variety, Margaret Duross, is one of the largest-flowered. Its tall, brittle flower stems need staking to be kept erect. Where a decorative wall or fence is not available to hide the lower foliage, plant a bushy perennial such as chrysanthemums.

Tuberous dahlias and gladiolus combine for a vibrant floral display that continues until fall frosts. To ensure a succession of bloom from dahlias, keep the faded flowers picked. For gladiolus, make succession plantings of corms at two-week intervals from early spring until midsummer.

Autumn crocus (*Colchicum byzantinum*) is a hardy, easy-to-grow perennial bulb that will bloom through turf if you peel back sections of grass, plant the bulbs in loose soil, and then firm the grass back in place. Autumn crocus blooms in late summer or early fall after the leaves have died away. While the leaves are green, they must not be mowed.

Instead of cutting spent flower stems to the ground at the onset of fall frost, let them develop decorative seed heads. The erect, dried seed-heads of *Rudbeckia hirta* (right) contrast with the arching leaves of eulalia grass (*Miscanthus sinensis* 'Variegatus'). A dusting of frost also adds an appealing quality to *Sedum* 'Autumn Joy' (foreground).

▶

Fall-blooming chrysanthemums are mostly seen planted formally in sunny beds and borders. For a change of pace, use them informally as this gardener did. Here, mums add color along a stream bank, where the presence of morning mists helps to soften their bright colors. The soil has been mounded along the bank to give the plants good drainage.

▼

In mild-winter areas, the autumn season is not as noticeable as in places with hard frosts. The tender perennial white-flowering succulent *Crassula* 'Campfire', with its orange and red leaves, establishes a beautiful autumnal appearance in a warm climate. It grows here in the company of ornamental grasses.

◀

For a change from the reds, golds, and oranges most common in autumn flower gardens, you can use these flowers in pink, white, and silver tones. Left to right are pale New England asters, deep-pink false dragonhead (*Physostegia virginica*), white pearly everlasting (*Anaphalis triplinervis*), pink Japanese anemone (*Anemone* x *hybrida*), white *Boltonia asteroides*, and lavender-blue *Ageratum coelestinum*.

For the most colorful winter berries, plant winterberry (*Ilex verticillata*). With the possible exception of firethorn (*Pyracantha coccinea*), no berry-bearing shrub has as bright a display. A deciduous holly, it loses its leaves in early autumn and carries its bright red berry clusters well into winter. Tolerant of moist soil, it is native to the Eastern Seaboard.

Winter aconites (*Eranthis hyemalis*) bloom in late winter, as early as do snowdrops. Even when covered with snow, the flowers will simply close up and wait for a thaw. Here, the heat of their stems and leaves is melting a light covering of snow, and the flowers are beginning to unfold.

Snowdrops are easy to grow and delightful in late winter. They will naturalize freely in humus-rich soil in the light shade of deciduous trees. Here, a colony of snowdrops (*Galanthus nivalis*), triggered into bloom by a brief warming spell, waits patiently for the sun to shine and melt the light covering of snow that fell during the night.

If you love Christmas rose (*Helleborus niger*) but find that it will not grow for you, try Lenten rose (*Helleborus orientalis*) instead. Lenten roses, shown here, are much more widely adaptable than Christmas roses. They bloom a bit later than their relative, but still very early in the year.

▼

Gazebos make good winter garden accents, especially in a woodland setting where snow will accentuate their decorative architectural lines. The dried beech leaves, the ground-covering evergreen *Pachysandra terminalis,* and a stepping-stone path are also accentuated by a light snowfall.

▶

Evergreen perennials and evergreen shrubs are vital to provide structure and interest during winter. This snow-covered garden offers an example of good structure, what landscape architects refer to as "good bones." The beds and borders are defined by yew, boxwood, and ivy, separated by brick paths. The contrasting spiky leaves of hardy evergreen perennial *Yucca filamentosa* provide an eye-catching foliage accent in the foreground bed.

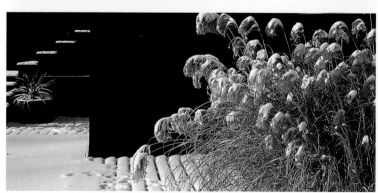

▲

Perennial maiden grass (*Miscanthus sinensis*) has flowers that dry and persist through winter. The slender, arching leaves shed snow with ease, but the nodding seedheads catch the snow, presenting decorative cottony plumes. When a spring thaw begins, cut the old leaves and stems to the ground so that new growth can develop without hindrance.

▲

A strong design evokes a sense of classic beauty, even in the dead of winter when the perennials are all dormant, hidden beneath a blanket of snow. This formal garden is structured by beds outlined in boxwood, a Colonial-style criss-cross fence, English teak benches, and a trelliswork arbor with seats.

◄ Wherever winters are mild, as in Florida and Southern California, florist's cyclamen (*Cyclamen persicum*) is spectacular for outdoor bedding. In the northern states, the plants are injured by freezing, but potted plants will bloom for a long time in a cool greenhouse, conservatory, or sunroom.

◄ Spring-flowering bulbs, such as daffodils, hyacinths, calla lilies, and tulips, can be purchased in bud from local growers to bloom indoors during the winter months, and can then be planted in the garden. Early blooming occurs indoors after the bulbs have experienced a cold, dark period, usually ten weeks in pots.

▲ In frost-free areas such as Florida and Southern California, that Christmas poinsettia received as a gift can be removed from its pot and planted outdoors to rebloom during the winter months. This eye-catching clump decorates a corner of a community garden devoted mostly to growing vegetables.

▶ Even in winter dormancy, many kinds of ornamental grasses look beautiful. Here, weeping brown sedge (*Carex flagelifera*), covers a slope at Western Hills Garden in Occidental, California, contrasting its beige-colored leaves with a grove of evergreen blue spruce and a pink winter-flowering heath.

Chapter Six

Perennials of Distinction

In the world of perennials, there are special plant families that are consistently sought after for their spectacular flowers, or for other endearing qualities such as beautiful foliage or graceful form. The following elite list includes both hardy and tender perennials. Those that are tender are popular not only in mild-winter areas, such as Southern California and the Gulf States, but also as container plants, sheltered indoors over winter in the northern states.

Cactus

Most cacti are tender perennials, though one species of hardy prickly pear (*Opuntia humifusa*) is native to the Northeast and is sufficiently hardy to survive freezing winters into Canada.

Cacti can be classified as desert cacti (preferring full sun and tolerating drought) and jungle cacti (preferring light shade and regular amounts of water). Desert cacti have interesting sculptural forms (such as barrel shapes and serpentlike stems that snake over the ground) plus sharp spines that add decorative qualities when they are viewed from a distance. Many desert cacti have beautiful flowers, in every color except blue, and they are exquisite when planted in contrasting groups among rock outcrops, especially in combination with desert succulents, such as *Kalanchoe, Euphorbia, Agave,* and *Aloe* species.

Jungle cacti (such as the Christmas cactus) have flattened, straplike stems composed of fleshy segments that hang down. In homes and frost-free gardens, they are beautiful plants to display in hanging baskets. The orchid cactus (*Epiphyllum* species) and fragrant night-blooming cereus (*Selenicereus grandiflora*), with blooms up to ten inches across, are especially striking.

Chrysanthemums and Asters

(*Chrysanthemum* and *Aster* species.) What tulips are to springtime, asters and chrysanthemums are to autumn. Nothing among perennials can match the color range of chrysanthemums in autumn. Developed from species of asters native to Asia, particularly China, the modern chrysanthemum (commonly called *cushion mum*) also includes a vast range of flower forms, including daisy-flowered, spider-flowered (displaying quilled petals), spoons (with upward-curled petals), and pompon (or button) types. Colors include yellow, orange, red, pink, purple, bronze, and white, plus bicolors.

Most chrysanthemums are purchased in a ready-to-bloom stage at local nurseries and are used just one time, massed for autumn display, but many are hardy and will survive winter to rebloom. A particularly good hardy strain is the Fantasias. Chrysanthemums are good to use not only as a rainbow border, but also in containers, and to add to odd corners of mixed perennial borders where there are gaps of color.

Perhaps the best-loved members of the daisy family, asters are also fall blooming and are derived from selections and crosses involving two North American species: the New England aster (*Aster novae-angliae*) and the New York aster (*Aster novi-belgii*). Both are common wayside plants in eastern North America, from Nova Scotia to Alabama. The New England aster, with violet-purple flowers, is most commonly seen in the wild.

Asters are extremely hardy and easy to grow. They can be transplanted at any time of the year when the ground is not frozen and tolerate a wide range of soil conditions, from dry to moist, as long as they receive sunlight. You can easily increase them by dividing up the roots every three years, and they are rarely bothered by pests or diseases. As to design, they fit into most mixed perennial borders, especially planted beside white boltonia, pink Japanese anemones, silvery lamb's ears, fountain grass, and Autumn Joy sedum. Asters look sensational planted along split-rail fences or picket fences, and the fencing helps to hold the stems erect. The tall kinds are also excellent for cutting.

Daffodils

(*Narcissus* species and hybrids.) Native to Europe, particularly the Pyrenees mountains and the Alps, daffodils can be used on a small scale, planted in containers or tucked into odd corners of the garden, and they can be used on a massive scale, to cover huge sections of woodland or meadow.

Daffodils like a humus-rich soil and either full sun or light shade. The bigger the bulb, the better the bloom, so be sure to buy only "top-size" bulbs. When planting, cover the bulbs with six inches of soil. Though they should be planted as soon after September 1 as possible, planting can be delayed until Christmas or until the ground freezes. Late planting will simply delay their spring bloom by two or three weeks. To keep daffodil bulbs coming back, always allow the leaves to die down naturally. Cutting the leaves will deplete the bulb of energy. Feeding with a high-phosphorus fertilizer is also beneficial.

Though shades of yellow predominate, white is common, and many of the most eye-catching daffodils have deep orange-red trumpets. There are also double-flowered kinds that are highly fragrant. Daffodils are extremely hardy, to Zone 3, and although they need a prolonged chilling period to come back, they can be grown in frost-free areas if they are stored in the vegetable bin of a refrigerator for eight weeks before being transferred to the garden in January.

Daylilies

(*Hemerocallis* species and hybrids.) Daylilies are to summer what daffodils are to spring. They seem to tolerate every kind of difficult climatic condition and planting site with the exception of boggy soil and deep shade. They survive high heat and drought better than most other perennials, and by selecting modern hybrids, you can have a floral display that lasts several months. Their hardiness range extends from Zone 3 to Zone 10; daylilies do well even in Florida and Southern California.

The wild daylily (*Hemerocallis fulva*) seen along the waysides of North America is an immigrant from China. Its beautiful, tawny, trumpet-shaped blooms last several weeks. Planted on slopes, it effectively controls soil erosion, but for garden display, consider only hybrid varieties.

Fragrant daylilies are scarce, but one of the best is Hyperion, a large, lemon-yellow variety. Daylilies are so carefree that you can buy them from nurseries in full bloom to create a rainbow border of exactly the color tones you want. They have fleshy, tuberous roots that can be divided after three years. They are indispensable in mixed perennial borders, since the color range is so extensive. Use them around pools so the leaves cascade into the water, and mass them informally to create meadow plantings.

Hibiscus

(*Hibiscus* species.) Most people think of hibiscus as tender tropical plants, exemplified by *Hibiscus rosa sinensis*, which flaunts large, eight-inch blooms in vibrant colors: red, yellow, orange, pink, and white. They are ever-blooming in frost-free locations, and in the northern states, are good for decorating patios and decks, planted in tubs that can be moved under glass in winter. However, there are many hardy hibiscus that are even larger flowered than the tropical kinds, such as *Hibiscus moscheutos* 'Southern Belle'. Its red, white, and pink flowers measure up to ten inches across.

Southern Belle flowers the first year from seed, and though the young seedlings are sensitive to frost damage, the roots of mature plants are hardy and will survive freezing to rebloom each year from midsummer to fall frost.

Growing to five feet high and equally wide, just one plant of Southern Belle can make a spectacular lawn highlight, with up to twenty dinner-plate-size blooms opening all at one time. These plants tolerate boggy soil and are especially beautiful when planted along stream banks and pond margins in the company of cardinal flowers (*Lobelia cardinalis*).

Ice Plants

(*Drosanthemum* and *Lampranthus* species.) Native to South Africa's semidesert areas, the low, spreading, succulent ice plants are mostly tender perennials that bloom in early spring. All have daisylike flowers and iridescent petals. The flowers are sometimes so profuse that they may completely hide the foliage, opening around 10 A.M. and closing around 4 A.M. on sunny days. Mostly used in Southern California for low bedding and for covering slopes, ice plants are tolerant of both salt spray and poor, sandy soil.

Drosanthemums are mostly pink-flowered, and *Lampranthus* species may be red, yellow, orange, or bicolored. Closely related to them are *Carpobrotus* species (Hottentot figs). They are large-flowered—up to five inches across—and the most salt-tolerant and drought-tolerant of all ice plants. A yellow form (*Carpobrotus edulis*) is native to South Africa, but a more beautiful, rosy-pink one (*Carpobrotus chiloensis*) is native to coastal Chile and also parts of coastal California. They are suitable for stabilizing shifting sand.

There are several hardy species of ice plants suitable for northern gardens, mostly species of *Delosperma*, in yellow, white, and carmine red. Used for edging and decorating dry walls, they are reliably hardy from Zone 6 south.

Iris

(*Iris* species.) There are more than 150 species of iris worldwide, growing from rhizomes or bulbous rootstocks. Many are tolerant of moist soil (such as the Siberian iris, *Iris sibirica*), and some (such as Japanese iris, *Iris ensata*) will thrive with their roots permanently immersed in water. However, bearded iris are the showiest of all, and they demand a well-drained soil in full sun. They are extremely drought-tolerant and will grow anywhere in North America except Alaska, Hawaii, and south of Orlando, Florida.

The color range of bearded iris is exceptional—one of the most extensive in the plant kingdom. The most common colors include blue, yellow, red, pink, orange, and white, but there are also black, green, and bicolored irises. The petal colors are usually enhanced by a contrasting "beard": a prominent cluster of yellow or orange stamens extending from the throat. Peak color occurs in late spring. Grow bearded iris in mixed perennial borders, or as a rainbow border packed solid with iris varieties in different color groups.

Lilies

(*Lilium* species and hybrids.) The true family of lilies is a diverse group with a blooming period that extends from late spring to early autumn, depending on variety. Not all lilies deserve their reputation of being difficult to grow, particularly the tiger lily (*Lilium lancifolium*) and some of the Asiatic hybrids, such as Mid-Century hybrids. This group offers a beautiful color mixture. When you buy a "naturalizing mixture" of lilies, it is usually the Mid-Century hybrids that are offered.

All garden lilies thrive in a humus-rich, well-drained soil. They should be fertilized after flowering so the bulb can replenish itself and rebloom next year. Lilies are valuable for decorating lightly shaded areas, especially on slopes. They tolerate full sun, as long as their roots are shaded, and they are valuable for cutting.

Maiden Grasses

(*Miscanthus* species.) When planning to use ornamental grasses in a garden, it's important to realize that their color variation is extensive, not only in their beautiful flowers, but also in their leaves, which may be bright red, bright blue, yellow, bronze, or white, as well as many shades of green. It's good to start with the hardy maiden grasses (*Miscanthus* varieties), as they tend to be the dominant plants. They are not as tall as some of the giant reeds and pampas plumes, but they are bulky, with masses of slender, arching leaves that rustle and shimmer in the slightest breeze.

Though ornamental grasses can be used with other perennials to soften herbaceous borders, consider devoting a garden space entirely to ornamental grasses, planted for subtle foliage effects.

Few categories of herbaceous perennials are as carefree as maiden grasses and the related ornamental grasses. Most tolerate long periods of drought, and by a proper selection of varieties, it's possible to find useful kinds suitable for just about any difficult planting site, including dry slopes and pure sand.

New Zealand Flax

(*Phormium tenax.*) New Zealand flax is a magnificent foliage plant displaying pointed, straplike, evergreen leaves in a fountainlike effect. There are two species in cultivation, plus a host of hybrids. All are tender and are best suited for Zone 8 and south. However, they are easily overwintered in the northern states when grown in containers and moved indoors during winter.

The New Zealand flaxes are drought-tolerant and survive a wide range of temperature extremes, though they will freeze when subjected to prolonged cold spells below 20 degrees F. In desert conditions, they may suffer sun scald unless planted in bright shade. Color stability among the hybrids may vary. In some of the more exotic bicolor and tricolor varieties, the original color can be maintained by removing old foliage to force new growth.

Hostas

(*Hosta* species and hybrids.) Hostas, or plantain lilies, are now such a popular shade plant that they rival daylilies, irises, and peonies in their frequency of use.

Though hostas are valuable for shade, tolerating even dense shade, in the Northeast they relish sun, provided the soil has a high humus content to help keep the roots cool. In the southern states, ample moisture and shade are essential for good results.

Most varieties are hardy from Zones 3 to 9. In addition to displaying magnificent foliage colors (particularly blue, gold, lime green, and bicolors), many display beautiful flower clusters with trumpet-shaped blooms as conspicuous as foxgloves. Fragrance is often an added bonus, especially in the varieties Royal Standard and Honey Bells.

Hostas make excellent groundcovers, especially along woodland walks. If you combine different leaf colors and textures, you can create a "tapestry" effect.

Because hostas lose their leaves in winter and don't break dormancy until later spring, they are excellent companions for bulbs, covering over dead bulb foliage after the bulb display has finished. They like a moist soil and look sensational bordering streams and ponds. In dry, sandy soil or heavy clay soil, dig in lots of garden compost, leaf mold, or peat to improve the soil's humus content.

Peonies

(*Paeonia* species.) There are two kinds of peony popular in American gardens: the herbaceous peony (*Paeonia officinalis*), which blooms mostly in early June, and the larger-flowered tree peony (*Paeonia suffuticosa*),which blooms mostly in mid-May. Both are hardy from Zones 5 to 9, though the herbaceous peony needs a longer winter chilling period than the tree peony. Both grow in sun or light shade and prefer a humus-rich, fertile loam soil, but the tree peony likes its roots to be sheltered.

Herbaceous peonies form mounded clumps up to four feet high, producing mostly rounded, fragrant flowers up to six inches across in crimson, pink, white, and bicolors. After a shower of rain, the flowers may become so heavy that they bend to the ground unless supported. The beautiful dark green indented leaves die to the ground after frost. Herbaceous peonies are good companions for Oriental poppies and bearded irises in mixed perennial borders, but they also can be planted with tree peonies to form a peony garden.

Tree peonies may grow to ten feet high, though most varieties will stay below six feet. They form woody stems that persist all winter, but lose their leaves after frost.

Phlox

(*Phlox* species.) There are more than 60 species of phlox, most of them hardy, and most of them native to North America. Varieties such as mountain pinks (*Phlox subulata*) and shade-tolerant blue phlox (*Phlox divaricata*) are low, spreading plants that bloom in early spring.

Summer phlox is the showiest, growing strong, erect stems topped with massive flower clusters that may measure up to eight inches across. Colors include white, pink, lavender-blue, and red; many varieties have a contrasting color zone at the center of each flower. Summer phlox makes a good component of mixed borders, especially in combination with hollyhocks and daylilies. Its only sin is a susceptibility to powdery mildew disease, which discolors the foliage. Some mildew-resistant varieties are available, such as Eva Cullum, a beautiful pink. Phlox maculata 'Alpha' (a deep rose-pink) flowers a week or two earlier than summer phlox, and its foliage is mildew-resistant.

In full sun and a well-drained, fertile loam soil, summer phlox will form thick clumps and benefits from division after three years. The tall kinds may need staking.

Poppies

(*Papaver* species.) Blooming mostly in spring, Oriental poppies have ephemeral flowers that are easily susceptible to wind and rain damage, but the large, shimmering petals can outshine everything else in the garden, and in a sheltered location, they may last a week.

Hardy into Canada, Oriental poppies are most effective massed in beds and borders or grown in generous clumps among bearded irises and herbaceous peonies. They grow to four feet high and may need staking to keep the stems erect.

Iceland poppies (*Papaver nudicaule*) are hardy perennials that burn up in summer heat, and so they are grown mostly as annuals. However, in coastal California gardens and in high-elevation areas where summers stay cool, the faded flower stems can be cut back, and the leafy rosettes will live on to flower another season.

Himalayan poppies (*Meconopsis* species) are temperamental plants that detest hot, dry summers. The famous blue poppy (*Meconopsis grandis*) does well only in the Pacific Northwest.

Sages

(*Salvia* species.) *Salvia* is a large genus of hardy and tender perennials undemanding about soil. Its most famous member is common sage (*Salvia officinalis*), a culinary herb with aromatic, decorative gray-green leaves and beautiful blue flower spikes, suitable for planting in mixed flower borders as well as herb gardens.

Some sages are grown primarily for their decorative foliage effect; one of them is *Salvia argentea*, which forms a large rosette of woolly silver leaves like lamb's ears (*Stachys byzantina*), but larger. Sages excel in bright red and deep blue flowers.

Sedums

(*Sedum* species.) The drought-tolerant succulent sedums include low, ground-hugging forms, such as Dragon's-blood (*Sedum spurium*), and erect, clump-forming types, such as stonecrop (*Sedum spectabile*). Both of these have beautiful star-shaped flowers that are attractive to butterflies, but other sedums are noted for colorful leaves, such as bronze (*Sedum maximum* 'Atropurpureum'), blue (*Sedum seiboldii*), and red (the tender *Sedum rubrotinctum*).

The autumn-flowering hybrid *Sedum* 'Autumn Joy' is one of the ten most popular hardy perennials, principally because its dome-shaped flower heads are decorative for several months. They start off white while in bud, open out to deep pink, mature to a dark red, and dry to a chestnut-brown. Unlike one of its parents, *Sedum spectabile*, the flower head of Autumn Joy holds together for a long time after frost and remains attractive, especially when planted close to the amber leaf blades and dried seedheads of ornamental grasses.

Tulips

(*Tulipa* species and hybrids.) Some of the wild species tulips, such as the waterlily tulips (*Tulipa kaufmanniana*) and candlestick tulips (*Tulipa clusiana*), will naturalize freely, coming back year after year. But many of the highly hybridized varieties, such as the Triumph tulips and Darwin hybrids, deteriorate quickly after the second season. For the best quality of tulip display, it's best to start with new bulbs every second year, planting in autumn (at any time after September 1) in a sunny or lightly shaded humus-rich soil.

Tulips have the the most intense colors and the widest color range of any perennial. Many interesting flower forms are available, including lily-flowered, peony-flowered, and fringe-flowered.

Use species tulips as drifts in rock gardens and for edging rustic paths. Use the hybrids for mass bedding, and as clumps in mixed perennial borders.

Waterlilies

(*Nymphaea* species.) Waterlilies, summer-flowering aquatic plants, can be planted singly in a water-filled whiskey half-barrel to provide a terrace or patio accent, or to decorate a pond or pool. There are two kinds to consider: hardy and tropical. Hardy waterlilies can remain below the ice level of a pond all winter, but the tropicals must spend the winter under glass, except in frost-free areas.

In small ponds and pools, it's best to grow waterlilies in submerged tubs, and to sink the container at least twelve inches below the water surface. The soil should be a fertile clay loam with compost mixed in. Waterlilies are heavy feeders and benefit from having fertilizer tablets pressed into the soil around their roots once a month until the middle of August.

The tropical waterlilies are larger than the hardies, and some have magnificent mottled leaves, together with a heady fragrance, but they can be temperamental. If your pond or pool is spring-fed, it's unlikely they will succeed, since they need higher temperatures than hardy waterlilies (preferably above 70 degrees F). Also, the temperature should be stable; tropical waterlilies don't like fluctuating temperatures. There is a misconception that the tropicals do not bloom as long as the hardies, but actually, the hardies generally dwindle by the beginning of September, while tropicals may continue flowering for another four weeks, until frost.

◄ ▲

Cactus gardens need excellent drainage and a soil that contains gritty soil particles, so it pays to establish specially prepared raised beds, like this one. The golden coloring of rotund barrel cactus (*Echincocactus grusonii*), in the foreground, contrasts effectively with the silvery variegated swordlike leaves of succulent century plants (*Agave americana*).

A bench-top collection of potted cacti in a greenhouse features exotic flowers and bizarre forms to evoke a living desert landscape in miniature. A key to flowering is a rest period during the winter months when the plants receive less water and no fertilizer. A regular watering and fertilizing schedule that begins in early March promotes flowering during spring and early summer.

◄

A group of succulent plants called *stonecrops* thrives in shallow soil. This tender perennial variety, *Echeveria elegans*, has been used to roof a tool shed. A layer of chicken wire stapled to the roof overhang is used to hold an inch of peaty soil to the roof. In severe winter climates, hen-and-chickens (*Echeveria* species) serves as a hardy substitute.

◄

Many kinds of cacti grow thick, tall stems that can be used as living sculpture. Here, silver and golden forms of desert cacti contrast with the yellow-green leaves of a California live oak, the gray-green leaves of a European olive, and the blue-green leaves of a century plant in a California garden. A mass of yellow torchlike cacti, *Trichocereus spachianus*, glows in reflected sunlight.

◄

Fall-blooming New England asters (*Aster novae-angliae*) are mostly tall-growing and generally need support. Planting them against a fence is an easy way to help them stay erect.

◄

A bed of fall-blooming cushion chrysanthemums (*Chrysanthemum* × *morifolium*) combines two colors—Buckeye (red) and Orange Cushion—around a clump of maiden grass (*Miscanthus sinensis*) in a formal island bed. These chrysanthemums were grown from cuttings, held in nursery beds until flower buds formed, and then transplanted. Cushion mums need to be sheared several times early in the growing season to keep them compact.

◄

Special cascading kinds of fall-blooming chrysanthemums are delightful grown in containers to tumble from balconies and window boxes. In this southern garden, a cascading mum contrasts its daisylike flowers with the lustrous jade green foliage of a camellia.

▲

Hardy asters are excellent plants for "wild" gardens. Asters and chrysanthemums are members of the same plant family, but asters tend to retain more of a wild, less hybridized appearance that is better suited to informal borders and natural landscapes. This beautiful informal planting of midsummer- to fall-blooming asters (*Aster* × *frikartii* 'Monch') decorates a rocky slope.

▶

The marguerite daisy (*Argyranthemum frutescens*) is a tender spring-flowering perennial that works quite well in containers. Northern gardeners can treat marguerites as annuals; they will bloom for much of the summer if deadheaded regularly. In this California garden, a dome of white marguerites decorates a brick patio, along with a hanging basket of rose-pink ivy-leaf geraniums, potted florist's cyclamen, tulips, and daffodils.

Daffodils love the humus-rich soils of deciduous woods. This woodland path at Lenteboden Bulb Garden near New Hope, Pennsylvania, displays a choice selection of daffodil varieties each spring, for evaluation and sale. The yellow-and-orange bicolored variety, Duke of Windsor, is one of the most popular for naturalizing.

Paperwhite narcissus is highly fragrant and is extremely easy to flower indoors at Christmas to fill a room with its gardenialike perfume. In mild-winter areas, such as coastal California and the Gulf States, it will naturalize outdoors. Where the soil freezes during winter, hardy fragrant poet's daffodils (*Narcissus poetaz*) are good substitutes.

Hostas and narcissus are surprisingly compatible. Not only do young variegated hosta leaves look good next to this planting of *Narcissus* 'Ceylon', but the hosta leaves will grow to hide the dead daffodil foliage. At spring flower shows, the daffodil variety Ceylon consistently wins more awards than any other daffodil. It is also popular for cutting.

Daffodils make superb pot plants in both cool and warm climates. At this California home, a Mexican handcart holds pots of an exquisite pink-cupped variety, Rainbow. Though daffodils demand freezing winters to come back each year, California growers can use artificial refrigeration to condition the bulbs for flowering in pots.

Though most daffodil varieties have finished flowering by the time the main tulip displays begin, the flowering of daffodils can be delayed several weeks if they are planted late—at Christmas and even in January if the ground is not frozen. This formal bed of the variety Flower Record blooms well from a deliberate late planting.

▶

Masses of daylilies make a marvelous summer-flowering meadow. There is a wealth of daylilies for gardeners to choose among. Over 32,000 daylily varieties are registered in North America, and 12,000 are still in commerce. The Siloam hybrids featured in this photograph are the work of Pauline Henry, an Arkansas breeder.

▼

One of the most attractive "eyed" bicolor hybrid daylilies is Sure Thing, which is yellow with a conspicuous red zone. Not only does its unusual coloration stand out in a crowd, but its size is spectacular—almost as large as Christmas amaryllis!

◀

Daylilies can look spectacular in a bed all to themselves. Here, a mixed bed of daylilies is backed by a perennial border featuring pink meadow foam, blue Russian sage, and purple loosestrife. Surprisingly, there are no daylilies native to the Americas. All hybrids are from parents found growing wild in Asia, mostly Siberia, China, and Japan.

A low-maintenance rainbow border features an assortment of modern daylily hybrids. Though each flower lasts only a day, the flower stalks contain a cluster of up to 50 flower buds, sometimes more, so that an attractive floral display may last for almost two months. By selecting early, midseason, and late varieties, it's possible to have a daylily display from late spring until fall frost.

Siloam Ethel Smith is one of the best hybrid daylilies from the prolific hybridizer Pauline Henry. Though shy-flowering the first season after transplanting, it flowers abundantly once established. Plant it next to a sunny bench or patio so its gorgeous raspberry tones can be fully appreciated.

Daylilies combine beautifully with other perennials. This superb early-summer display features daylilies Peach Duet (foreground) and golden yellow Stella de Oro (rear). Vivid pink *Phlox maculata*, light pink *Oenothera speciosa*, and a lavender-blue *Salvia officinalis* harmonize with the warm-toned daylilies to create a bright display.

The orange wayside daylily, also known as the tawny daylily, is prolific throughout the eastern and midwestern United States; it's an escapee from gardens planted by early colonists. Incredibly, the flowers themselves are sterile, and the plant can spread only by pieces of root. It makes a virile, weed-suffocating groundcover, especially useful on sunny slopes to control soil erosion.

Though the old daylily variety Hyperion is famous for its large yellow trumpetlike blooms and delightful fragrance (a rare quality among daylilies), its flowering display is relatively short-lived. Patio Parade, planted here in an island bed, is barely distinguishable from Hyperion, but it is longer-blooming and also pleasantly fragrant.

▲

Hardy perennial geraniums form low mounds of sparkling color in perennial beds. *Geranium sanguineum* 'Lancastriense' (light pink) and *Geranium sanguineum* 'Shepherd's Warning' (rose pink) work beautifully together. In this garden, a carpet of *Sedum kamtschaticum*, bearing orange-flushed yellow flowers, unifies the foreground planting.

▼

Use ivy-leaf geraniums (*Pelargonium peltatum*) to create a curtain of color. Here, they are grown in pots and hanging baskets to create a solid mass of vibrant pink and red tones at a weekend cottage. Though ivy-leaf geraniums are treated as annuals where winters are freezing, they can be overwintered in frost-free locations and also under glass.

►

Don't be afraid to use a small patch of contrasting color when mixing flowering perennials. The magenta Armenian cranesbill (*Geranium psilostemon*) strikes a dramatic note when combined with the yellow loosestrife and orange lilies in the background; it is an appealing contrast. The plants can be allowed to spill informally into pathways, as here, or they can be supported by bamboo stakes to grow into erect clumps.

►

Scented-leaf geraniums generally have inconspicuous flowers. However, the leaves not only are pleasantly fragrant but offer beautiful shapes, textures, and subtle shades of green. Here, the velvety scalloped leaves of the rose-scented geranium (*Pelargonium graveolens*) contrast appealingly with the indented silvery leaves of the nutmeg-scented geranium (*P. fragrans*).

For a dramatic planting try the hardy hybrid hibiscus, Southern Belle (*Hibiscus moscheutos*). Hybridized from swamp mallows, which are native to the Northeast, this plant blooms non-stop from mid-summer to fall frost. Tolerant of moist soil and good for pond settings, it combines well here with annual pink spider flower (left) and perennial cardinal flowers (rear).

Tender tropical hibiscus (*Hibiscus rosa-sinensis*) can be grown outdoors in frost-free areas such as Florida and Southern California. In this raised bed surrounding a palm tree, bright red and yellow hybrids shine among clumps of shrimp plant (*Beloperone guttata*). In the northern states, tropical hibiscus and shrimp plant are easy to grow in pots that are overwintered indoors.

The hardy white-flowering form of *Hibiscus moscheutos* 'Southern Belle' is a terrific accent or background plant in an all-white garden. Here, it thrives in the company of white annuals including zinnias, globe amaranth, spider flower, snow-on-the-mountain, and moonflower vine.

Though hybrids of *Hibiscus moscheutos* are hardy perennials, they will flower the first year from seed started indoors six weeks before outdoor planting. Flowering in midsummer, the plants continue blooming until frost. Here, they are used along a house foundation with perennial *Chrysanthemum* x *rubellum* 'Clara Curtis'.

Few perennials thrive among sand dunes as successfully as the yellow ice plant (*Maleophora crocea*), seen here in early spring in a drought- and salt-tolerant garden at Malibu Beach, California. White trailing African daisy (*Osteospermum frutescens*) and purple Hottentot fig (*Carpobrotus edulis*) flower closer to the shoreline.

A dry, sunny slope in a desert or coastal California climate is a congenial place for South African wildflowers. This planting includes orange ice plant (*Lampranthus aurantiacus*, a tender perennial), and annual African daisies.

The rosy ice plant, or dewflower (*Drosanthemum speciosum*), is most often seen in desert and coastal California gardens, planted in great sheets of iridescent color across dry slopes. Here, a small patch contrasts its brilliance with the slender, spiky leaves of a Mexican grass tree (*Dasylirion longissimum*) in a desert landscape that also includes species of cactus.

A carpet of drought-tolerant, pink-flowering Hottentot fig (*Carpobrotus edulis*) is a beautiful contrast to the silvery, decorative bark of a eucalyptus tree. Here, the duo occupy a sunny strip of sandy soil between a driveway and a wooded area. The shimmering flowers of Hottentot fig open only on sunny days between 10 A.M. and 4 P.M.

▲
Yellow flag iris (*Iris pseudacorus*) is good for boggy soil, even flowering with its roots permanently immersed in water. A large-flowered form of buttercup (*Ranunculus acris*) thrives in moist soil at its feet. The edges of this boggy area are decorated with clumps of hardy bamboo and maiden grass (*Miscanthus sinensis*).

▲
Bearded iris (*Iris* × *germanica*) are dominant in blues, and a mixed border may look bland unless it contains a good balance of oranges and yellows like this rainbow border. At the Presby Iris Garden in Montclair, New Jersey, commercially successful bearded iris varieties are arranged in beds according to their year of introduction. Bearded iris like a well-drained, fertile loam soil.

▶
These naturalized plantings of blue and white Siberian iris (*Iris sibirica*) are massed in a low-lying meadow that remains boggy for most of the winter. Siberian iris tolerates a wide range of conditions, including dry soil, though it is susceptible to rodent damage in soils with good drainage.

Japanese iris (*Iris ensata*) has flowers almost as large as bearded iris, but it displays its flowers in a flat-topped petal arrangement best viewed from above. This clump of purple-flowering hybrids has its roots covered with shallow water all year. Part of a Japanese garden, it is viewed from a footpath leading to a rustic gazebo (left).

Blue bearded iris looks sensational when viewed against a mass of silvery foliage and sprays of white flowers. Here, King of the Blues is accentuated by perennial artemisia foliage and perennial ox-eye daisies (*Leucanthemum vulgare*) in late spring.

Japanese iris are wonderful companions for ferns and hostas, as here along a woodland path. This variety, Nikko, is one of the most vigorous and largest flowered. The Japanese iris is the last iris to bloom; most varieties reach peak flowering by midsummer, but a few flower spikes may still occur into August.

Dwarf crested iris (*Iris cristata*) is one of the earliest flowering dwarf iris, blooming with yellow perennial alyssum and blue bugle weed, seen here beside a woodland path. Native to eastern woodland clearings, dwarf crested iris tolerates light shade, and it will quickly form sheets of blue in humus-rich soil. There is also a white variety.

Hardy perennial plantain lilies (*Hosta* species and hybrids) create a luxurious groundcover in the dappled shade of trees like this river birch. They are carefree foliage plants, and many have ornamental bell-shaped flowers in summer and autumn. Hostas are deciduous, dying down after frost and sprouting new shoots in spring. By the time the azaleas bloom, they are fully emerged.

There are hundreds of hosta species and hybrids to choose from. One of the best for blue-green coloration is Sea Foam. Though the large heart-shaped leaves resemble those of many other kinds of *Hosta sieboldiana* hybrids, Sea Foam has the best flowering display, especially in light shade.

Hostas and bog primulas make good companions, since they both like moist soil. Here, in early spring, along a small stream, the variegated cream-and-green leaves of *Hosta* 'Frances Williams' echo the yellow blooms of *Primula* x *bullesiana*, and the green part of the hosta leaves is a good foil for the pink and orange shades of the delicate primrose flowers.

A double line of hostas makes a handsome edging for a grass path leading to a woodland garden. The front row contains mostly solid green and green-variegated hostas. The back row contains exclusively blue-foliaged *Hosta sieboldiana*. A background of feathery evergreen Canadian hemlock provides a good contrast for both kinds of hostas.

Autumn-flowering *Hosta* 'Fall Bouquet' has small, narrow pointed leaves compared to most other varieties of hosta, but it has the advantage of beautiful late-blooming blue flowers that seem to sparkle in this shaded border edging a brick path. Developed by Long Island hosta hybridizer Paul Aden, it is a good visual contrast with the larger, variegated leaves of *Hosta sieboldiana* 'Frances Williams'.

Though hostas thrive in damp soil in partial shade, they will tolerate fairly dry, sunny positions, as here along a stepping-stone path that leads through sandy soil where thrift (*Armeria maritima*) flowers in spring. Though robust plants, hostas have a quiet dignity that complements many dwarf evergreen groundcovers, such as prostrate junipers and hardy sedums.

Many varieties of hosta have beautiful golden yellow autumnal leaf coloring; they are especially effective planted against a background of evergreen mosses. This is *Hosta sieboldiana* 'Aurea Marginata'; from the outer leaf margins, its foliage turns a golden yellow that accentuates vivid green leaf veins.

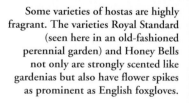

Some varieties of hostas are highly fragrant. The varieties Royal Standard (seen here in an old-fashioned perennial garden) and Honey Bells not only are strongly scented like gardenias but also have flower spikes as prominent as English foxgloves.

◀

The Asiatic hybrid *Lilium* 'Enchantment' is a popular garden lily because its orange color carries a long distance. Like most lilies, it grows long stems that need a screen of flowers or foliage to avoid looking leggy. Here, the bronze leaves of a barberry shrub hide and support the lily stems. Also sharing space in the border are blue *Nepeta* 'Six Hills Giant' and white *Filipendulina vulgaris*.

▼

The tiger lily (*Lilium lancifolium*) thrives in light shade, like that cast by a white birch. Not only does it increase by means of bulb division, but it forms black bulblets along its stems. After the plants have flowered in summer, the bulblets can be collected and planted to form new colonies.

◀

Oriental lilies have the largest flowers, especially selections of the gold-banded lily (*Lilium auratum*). Here, it towers above a perennial border in the company of purple loosestrife, its magnificent waxlike petals glowing in the light of a setting sun. The gold-banded lily was used in breeding Jan de Graaf's Imperial Strain, which includes pink and red in its color range.

◀

Garden lilies are mostly summer flowering, but this Asiatic lily, Endeavor, is so early flowering that it will bloom at the same time as late-flowering rhododendrons, such as Celeste, seen here. Both lilies and rhododendrons like humus-rich, acid soil and light shade.

The tall centerpiece in this spectacular grouping of hybrid lilies is Thunderbolt, a strong-growing orange trumpet lily that survives for 30 years or more. In the rear border are several excellent lily companions: pink meadow foam (*Limnanthes douglasi*), purple loosestrife, and blue Russian sage.

In warm climates where Asiatic and Oriental hybrid lilies will not grow well, try fragrant white trumpet lilies (*Lilium longiflorum*). They are tender perennials, mostly grown under glass as pot plants for sale as Easter lilies. But they will overwinter outdoors in frost-free coastal climates. This mass planting in an island bed is edged with annual alyssum.

Tall trumpet lilies are good companions for blue delphiniums. The lily varieties here are Pink Perfection and Black Dragon (so named because the white flowers are marked with maroon on the outside). Both are strong, disease-resistant hybrids developed by Jan de Graaff.

Mid-Century Hybrid lilies are almost as easy to grow as daffodils. Here, in the light shade of a Pennsylvania woodland garden, they have naturalized along the slopes of a stream, in company with hostas and ferns. The owner purchased five hundred bulbs the first year; when he saw how well they had grown, he added another thousand.

The very best maiden grass for autumn display is the variety *Miscanthus sinensis* var. *purpurascens*, also called *flame grass*. Its arching leaf blades start to turn reddish orange in September and later deepen to purple. Simultaneously, it produces masses of shimmering silvery flower plumes that create a startling highlight in the autumn landscape.

Maiden grasses (*Miscanthus sinensis*) are at their best in autumn. This planting shows the wide variation in leaf color and flower color available, including the variety *purpurascens* (with orange leaves and silver flowers) and the cultivars Morning Light (with slender silver flowers, on the left), Undine (with large silver flowers, on the right), and Gracillimus (with reddish flowers, in the rear).

New Zealand flaxes are good companions for species of *Miscanthus*, especially porcupine grass (*Miscanthus sinensis* 'Strictus'), here showing its magnificent reddish flower plumes and fountainlike green leaf blades flecked with yellow. In this poolside planting, it is in company with potted New Zealand flax and an edging of variegated ribbon grass (*Phalaris arundinacea* 'Picta').

Japanese silver grass (*Miscanthus sinensis* 'Variegatus') lights up a border in autumn and provides a handsome backdrop for other fall perennials. Clumps of rusty red *Sedum* 'Autumn Joy' echo the reddish flower plumes of the silver grass, while the broad, heart-shaped bright green leaves of *Hosta* 'Royal Standard' are a good contrast to the slender grass leaves.

Peonies are enchanting in a garden all by themselves. These red, pink, and white herbaceous peonies are planted in rectangular island beds cut into a grassy clearing in the woodland. Their bright, fragrant blooms are cherished as cut flowers.

Herbaceous peonies make spectacular flowering hedges during the growing season, and their indented foliage remains attractive when the plants are not in bloom. Bright, iridescent peony blossoms also blend especially well with bearded iris and Oriental poppies. These are large-flowered Estate Peonies, developed by the midwestern peony hybridizer Charles Klehm & Son.

Peonies are quite wonderful in mixed perennial borders, especially when seen against an expanse of lawn. In this garden, a bold clump of rose-pink herbaceous peonies, in the foreground, complements pink and red climbing roses scrambling over a fence and a tool shed in the background. Blue bellflower (*Campanula*) and a low hedge of variegated *Hosta* 'Thomas Hogg' add splashes of complementary color.

Tree peonies not only bloom earlier than herbaceous peonies but also have much larger flowers. The plants develop into small woody shrubs instead of dying to the ground in autumn. Here, the blooms of Red Moon are exquisite, contrasting with the weathered wood of a split-rail fence. Tree peonies are also sensational viewed against old stone walls.

If you want the largest herbaceous peony flowers, choose among varieties of Estate Peonies. This border features a representative selection. Pink-flowering *Rhododendron* 'Roseum Elegans' not only echoes the pink-flowering peonies but extends the color high above an evergreen boxwood hedge, which was planted to highlight the peony blossoms.

A single plant of Barrington Belle almost smothers itself in gorgeous deep red blossoms on long, strong stems. Normally, the dome of stamens at the center of an herbaceous peony blossom is golden yellow, but in Barrington Belle, it is a mixture of red and gold that adds greatly to the flowers' ornamental effect. This plant, like all peonies, is a heavy feeder and requires a humus-rich, fertile soil.

Herbaceous peony Ivory Jewel flaunts its big white poppylike blooms among clumps of white and blue Siberian iris. Though many herbaceous peonies have the rounded double flowers prized by flower arrangers, the singles are the largest flowers. This one offers the added appeal of a large central dome of golden yellow stamens resembling the yolk of an egg.

Moss pinks (*Phlox subulata*), also called mountain pinks, are spring-flowering hardy perennials that bloom in white, red, and pink, in addition to the lavender-blue seen here. This shade harmonizes beautifully with other spring flowers, such as the blue bugle weed in the foreground and the blue forget-me-nots in the rear of this rock garden. Yellow perennial alyssum provides a good color contrast.

The bold cone-shaped flower clusters of summer phlox (*Phlox paniculata* 'Eva Cullum') brighten a perennial border in which a prostrate juniper cascades down a retaining wall to form an evergreen curtain. Most summer phlox are susceptible to powdery mildew disease, which discolors their foliage, but Eva Cullum is resistant, staying clean into the autumn months.

Resembling summer phlox in appearance, but earlier flowering and mildew-resistant, *Phlox maculata* adds height to a mixed border featuring golden yellow Stella de Oro daylily, blue *Stachys macrantha*, and pink *Oenothera speciosa*. This phlox variety is Alpha; its deep rose-pink flowers bloom two weeks before those of summer phlox.

Wild blue phlox (*Phlox divaricata*) is native to eastern American woodlands. Tolerant of shade, it has creeping stems that will form a dense weave, quickly establishing a flowering groundcover that's ideal for edging woodland paths. In addition to several shades of blue, there is a beautiful white.

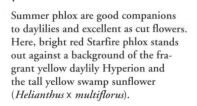

Clumps of summer phlox (*Phlox paniculata*) add an old-fashioned look to a midsummer perennial garden in New Hampshire. Summer phlox can be difficult to grow and tends to do better in New England than in other parts of the country. The top-heavy stems need tying in bundles to keep the flowers erect.

Summer phlox are good companions to daylilies and excellent as cut flowers. Here, bright red Starfire phlox stands out against a background of the fragrant yellow daylily Hyperion and the tall yellow swamp sunflower (*Helianthus* × *multiflorus*).

White and silver flowering perennials make good companions. Here, white mildew-resistant *Phlox maculata* 'Omega' creates a spectacular color harmony with silvery *Artemisia ludoviciana* 'Silver King' and the silvery blue indented foliage of cardoon (*Cynara cardunculus*).

Though prone to mildew disease in areas with hot, humid summers, summer phlox are mostly trouble-free in northeastern coastal gardens. This mixed border at historic Hunter House on the waterfront at Newport, Rhode Island, features a beautiful clump of summer phlox among perennial lavender, blue globe thistle, spirelike purple gayfeather, white spires of obedient plant, and yellow coreopsis. Vining annual nasturtiums weave a carpet of parasol leaves and red and orange flowers among the perennials, uniting the design.

Tender perennial New Zealand flax consists of two species and more than a hundred hybrids. The most commonly grown type, the coastal flax (*Phormium tenax*) tends to have stiff, erect sword-shaped leaf blades. This variety, Cream Delight, is a variegated form of the mountain species (*Phormium cookianum*), with an informal, carefree, tousled appearance.

The beautiful tricolored leaves of *Phormium tenax* 'Sunset' provide a strong foliage accent in a mixed border of red- and yellow-flowering perennials. It is seen here with yellow daylilies, yellow yarrow, red gazania, and red-hot poker (*Kniphofia uvaria*). The hot colors are softened by a clump of silvery *Artemisia* 'Powis Castle'.

There are many good bronze varieties of New Zealand flax. In this California hillside garden, the variety *purpureum* contrasts well with the silvery foliage and yellow flowers of yarrow and lavender cotton. In early spring, New Zealand flaxes produce tall woody flower stems valued by flower arrangers. Though the dull red flowers are inconspicuous, they are highly attractive to hummingbirds.

New Zealand flaxes are sensational planted in terra-cotta urns. This is *Phormium tenax* 'Sundowner', a tricolor variety with smooth olive-green sword-shaped leaves edged in pink. Here, it contrasts boldly with the feathery evergreen leaves of a dark green *Podocarpus* hedge in a small city garden in California.

Though *Salvia coccinea* 'Lady in Red' is a tender perennial, it will flower the first year from seed. Its bright red flower plumes are a welcome source of vertical line in a mixed border. They seem to sparkle in this garden, where the plant is established between a blue-mist shrub (*Caryopteris*), on the right, and clumps of white perennial baby's breath (*Gypsophila paniculata*).

This remarkable entrance garden, composed entirely of *Salvia* and closely related species, proves the versatility of this genus. Included in the design are yellow *S. forschaolii*, violet-blue *S. nemerosa*, pale blue *S. glutinosa*, and red *S. fulgens*. Blue English lavender and silvery lamb's ears are related to *Salvia*s. They are all members of the mint family.

Common sage (*Salvia officinalis*) is a culinary herb that is equally at home in perennial borders and herb gardens. The hardy perennial plants produce beautiful blue flowers in late spring. Here, the foliage colors of two variegated sages (golden sage and tricolor sage) create interesting patterns in the company of silvery lavender cotton.

Hardy violet sage *(Salvia × superba)* grows bushy plants with masses of violet-blue flowers. It is an outstanding companion for yellow flowers, especially *Coreopsis grandiflora.* The softer blue of *Campanula carpatica* tones down its intensity in this garden. Violet sage will bloom continuously all summer if the spent flower spikes are removed.

California has many tender wild sages that are drought-tolerant. One of the best is *Salvia clevelandii.* From it has been developed a beautiful hybrid variety, Alan Chickering, seen here in the company of yellow-flowering lavender cotton *(Santolina chamaecyparissus)* in a sunny California rock garden.

Gardeners need to be alert to unusual varieties of sages to make their perennial plantings more appealing, and to experiment with unfamiliar kinds. The vibrant rose-pink flowers in this flawless perennial border are from *Salvia fulgens.* It positively glows between clumps of *Canna* 'Elma Cole' and silvery *Artemesia ludoviciana* 'Silver King'.

◄

Autumn Joy is a hybrid of *Sedum spectabile*. The flowers open a deep rosy pink, mature to a deep rusty red, and turn chestnut brown when dry They are especially attractive planted with ornamental grasses, such as *Miscanthus sinensis*, which blooms at the same time. After frost, the amber autumn coloration of the grasses will complement the dried flower heads of Autumn Joy.

▲

Hardy perennial pink stonecrop (*Sedum spectabile*) is valuable not only for its late-summer flowers, but because it is highly attractive to butterflies, especially swallowtails and monarchs.

►

Many varieties of sedum are ground-hugging plants, suitable for edging. One of the best for summer is Dragon's-blood (*Sedum spurium*), here spilling its blood-red flowers over cushions of perennial Scotch and Irish mosses (*Arenaria* species) at the base of a rock garden.

In mild-winter areas such as Southern California, gardeners can use some of the spectacular giant sedums native to the Canary Islands. *Aeonium arboreum* not only grows huge evergreen rosettes of succulent leaves, even in sparse soil, but also has an attractive yellow flower spike that rises from the center in early summer. Here, it grows in the company of pansies and marguerite daisies.

Hen-and-chickens are hardy perennial sedums that are invaluable for dry, stony soils, where they will form large colonies by quickly producing offsets. Here, a bronze-leaf hybrid (*Sempervivum* x *fauconetti*) and a green-leaf species (*S. montana*) contrast their rosettes of succulent leaves with an evergreen Blue Rug juniper and the scalloped leaves of a dwarf yellow stonecrop (*S. kamtschaticum*).

This flagstone patio features a stone wall not only as a means of sheltering a collection of moisture-loving heathers on the inside of the wall, but also as a means of displaying a collection of drought-tolerant sedums planted along the top of the wall. Their evergreen leaves of different colors are decorative even after the plants have finished flowering.

▲

Iceland poppies (*Papaver nudicaule*) are hardy perennials that can be grown as hardy annuals, since they will flower the first year from seed if started early indoors. In most areas of North America, they burn up during hot summers and need replanting each year, but in cool coastal and high-elevation areas, the faded flower stems can be cut back so that the plants will bloom again.

▲

Oriental poppies (*Papaver orientale*) are good companions for bearded iris and ox-eye daisies, flaunting huge blooms with iridescent petals that resemble crepe paper. You can increase a particularly good color form, like this extra large scarlet, by chopping the fleshy roots into two-inch segments and replanting them.

▶

Look for perennial plants that can cascade down retaining walls to create an avalanche of blooms. The fragrant matilija poppy, or tree poppy (*Romneya coulteri*), is known as "queen of the California wild-flowers." It crosses with another California native (*R. tricocalyx*) to produce peony-size blossoms; the resulting tender hybrid perennials survive West Coast winters.

Oriental poppies (*Papaver orientale*) are sensational for sunny meadow plantings—especially the crimson and orange-red varieties, which catch the sunlight and create a blaze of color that can be seen from afar. This massed display, at the edge of a woodland, blooms faithfully each year in a Pennsylvania garden, where pink azaleas and pink-flowering dogwoods carry color into the tree canopy.

For a touch of class, consider the magnificent blue Himalayan poppy (*Mecanopsis grandis*). Though it will not tolerate hot summers, it succeeds as a perennial in the Pacific Northwest, where it blooms in late spring. Like rhododendrons, blue poppies demand a cool, lightly shaded, humus-rich soil. In the Northeast, they can be flowered in spring only from plants set into flowering positions each autumn.

Use the intense yellow of the hardy Welsh poppy (*Meconopsis cambrica*) to enliven areas planted with dark foliage. In this example, the background is filled with a bronze-leaf groundcover, *Ajuga reptans*. Rising above its bright green feathery foliage, the yellow poppy flowers appear to be fluttering butterflies.

◀ The light shade of a tree extends the blooming period of this beautiful color harmony of tulips, featuring Purissima (a white Fosteriana hybrid tulip), Peach Blossom (a rose-pink double-flowered tulip), and Mary Ann (an orange Greigii). When mixing varieties from different tulip classes, like these early-flowered kinds, it's important to be sure that they have the same blooming time.

▲ A bed of Darwin hybrid tulips follows the curve of a driveway at Lenteboden Bulb Garden in New Hope, Pennsylvania. Each color block represents a different variety. The Darwin hybrids are famous for large cup-shaped blooms and iridescent petals, achieved by crossing old Darwin tulips with *Tulipa fosteriana*.

▶ This award-winning small-space bulb garden features many bicolor tulip varieties. An underplanting of blue grape hyacinth (*Muscari armeniaca*) ties the design together. For a display like this, with every bulb producing a flower, it is essential to plant only "top-size" bulbs, since many cut-rate bulbs fail to flower the first year.

▶

It is not always a good idea to plant tulips for the gaudiest color combinations possible. This monochromatic planting of pale pink Douglas Bader tulips is in quiet harmony with the white trim on the surrounding structures, and also with the clump of white daffodils lining a path leading to a Victorian-style gazebo. The pale pastel color establishes a peaceful, understated, romantic quality.

▼

Because tulips offer the widest color range of all spring-flowering perennial bulbs, it is possible to create unusual analogous color harmonies, such as this mass planting featuring large drifts of black, purple, and lavender-blue Triumph tulips. It is a welcome change from the more common red-and-yellow tulip plantings.

▲

Many of the large double-flowered tulips make especially good potted plants. Here, terra-cotta planters are filled with Angelique, a pink-and-white bicolor that resembles a peony. In this arrangement, several pots of Angelique decorate a patio in company with pots of yellow trumpet daffodils and rose-pink florist's cyclamen.

To avoid a regimented look, put long-stemmed tulips together with early-flowering perennials. In this small-space rock garden planted beside a driveway, yellow leopard's bane (*Doronicum caudatum*), yellow crown imperials (*Fritillaria imperialis*), and glittering white foam flower (*Tiarella cordata*) and all good companions for a rich assortment of tulips.

Kaufmanniana hybrid tulips are commonly called "waterlily tulips" because they open their shimmering flowers out flat on sunny days, like a waterlily. The variety Stresa is an eye-catching, extra-early yellow-and-red bicolor, here planted between clumps of midseason tulips just starting to show buds.

Don't overlook the special charm of bicolor tulips. The red-and-white Garden Party in this informal bed of Triumph tulips seems to add sparkle in what might otherwise be a rather mundane mixture of solid colors. This planting is protected from damage by rodents by mixing moth repellant flakes among the bulbs at planting time the previous autumn.

Blocks of color from spring-flowering bulbs are generally more dramatic than a hodgepodge rainbow mixture. This red, yellow, and blue planting uses *Tulipa praestens* 'Red Fusilier' (a multi-flowered tulip) in the foreground, hyacinth Blue Jacket, Fosteriana hybrid tulip Red Emperor (rear) and yellow daffodils for a dazzling display.

Index